Choosing Childcare

Choosing Childcare

Nurseries, Registered childminders,
Nannies, Au pairs and Family

Elyssa Campbell-Barr

CPS

About the author

Elyssa Campbell-Barr has been researching and writing about quality childcare and education for over 15 years, as the award-winning editor of magazines for the National Childminding Association and the National Union of Teachers. Her work has also appeared in Nursery World magazine, on NetMums and in The Guardian, amongst others. Most importantly, she is a user of childcare herself, as the working mother of a three-year-old daughter and one-year-old son.

Elyssa is married to the author and illustrator Garen Ewing and lives in Sussex, where she now works as a freelance writer.

Choosing Childcare

Author: Elyssa Campbell-Barr
Managing Editor: Derek Cross
Consultant Editor: Mel Parks

ISBN: 978-0-9572680-5-0

 Cross Publishing Services

Printed by DG3 Group (Holdings) Ltd

For Garen, Miranda and Felix

With huge thanks to our childminder, Sue, staff at The Stables Nursery, and my mum and stepdad, Vanessa and John, without whose wonderful childcare this book would never have been written.

Acknowledgements

The author would like to thank the following individuals and organisations for their help and advice in compiling this book: Amy Mansell, former nursery deputy manager and Senco; Sarah Louise Porter, outstanding registered childminder, Peter Kemple Hardy of Every Disabled Child Matters; Gemma Oriel, proofreader and childminding expert; Dr Verity Campbell-Barr, lecturer in Early Childhood Studies at Plymouth University; The British Au Pair Agencies Association; The British Association of Professional Nannies; and my eagle-eyed dad, Bob Campbell-Barr. Thanks, too, to advisors from the Department for Education, Ofsted, the Care Inspectorate, Estyn and HMRC who answered our queries, to Dr Penelope Leach for her insightful foreword, and to Derek Cross who designed and published the book.

Last but not least, a special thank you to all the parents who were so generous in sharing their experiences of, and advice about, finding and using childcare.

Publisher's note

The publisher has made every effort to ensure the information in this book is correct at the time of printing (March 2016), but cannot guarantee its accuracy or completeness as regulations and government policies covering childcare and working parents change frequently and may vary in different parts of the UK. Financial information in particular may soon become outdated. Please check current regulations and guidance covering your area of the UK when making any decisions about childcare, or becoming, a working or studying parent.

The opinions and advice given in the quotes from parents do not necessarily reflect the opinions of the author or publisher and do not constitute recommendations. Mention of commercial companies does not constitute a recommendation or endorsement on the part of the author or publisher; nor is it advertising on the part of the company.

The publisher accepts no liability for any loss or damage arising from the use of or reliance on information in this book.

Updates, corrections and additional materials will be posted on the book's website: **www.choosing-childcare.co.uk** Password to access downloads: **childcare123**

Contents

Foreword

Dr Penelope Leach

One of the world's leading experts in child development and parenting, and bestselling author of *Your Baby and Child*, which has sold over two million copies.

Childcare is an emotionally loaded and uncomfortably complicated topic for almost every parent so the straightforward simplicity of this book is doubly welcome. *Choosing Childcare* tells you what kinds of childcare there are, how they compare with each other, how you might find them and what they might cost. Elyssa Campbell-Barr gives you an invaluable starting point into the maze of your childcare needs. In most families those needs are not a clear-cut either-or between one type of childcare and another, but a jigsaw puzzle of people and places, family and non-family, paid and unpaid, in the child's home, in someone else's home, or in a professional setting. To complicate matters further, not all non-maternal care is non-parental; there are increasing numbers of fathers caring for their children and even more fathers and mothers who want to share children's care, as well as some grandparents who want to spend time with children that's both useful and sociable.

Changing the way a child is cared for is never easy, and *Choosing Childcare* does not pretend that it is – or should be. But the book conveys a reassuring certainty that whatever hours or different types of childcare you plan on using, even a really clingy baby who has been used to having a parent home all the time through a year's leave will eventually take sympathetic daycare in his stride if you can give him enough time to adapt.

'Eventually' and 'sympathetic' are the key words in that sentence. Don't expect your baby to accept a new caregiver in a week, whether she's a nursery worker, a childminder or a nanny. He needs time to get to know her with you before he faces life with her and without you. If the new caregiver is in a new care-place – a nursery instead of home – perhaps the adaptation will be greater and take longer.

Do remember that settling with a caregiver means coming to love her. Changing caregivers does not just mean going through the getting-to-know-her process all over again; it also means losing somebody your child has become attached to. Of course, you cannot leave your baby with someone who proves unsuitable, but do use this book to choose as carefully as you possibly can in the first place. It's astonishing how many parents settle for a nursery on the basis of its lovely toys and tiny toilets without having met the people who work there or seen them with the children who will become their child's friends. It's even more amazing that nannies are hired without their references being actually checked. And although you cannot ask any individual caregiver to guarantee a long-term arrangement, do avoid those that are obviously temporary (like a childminder whose house is on the market or a nanny who plans to marry on another continent next year).

For some parents *Choosing Childcare* is wishful thinking because there is little affordable local choice available. The kind of person, setting and arrangement you can settle for depends primarily on who is already available, or could make themselves available, to care for the baby. If you wanted a nursery place but the only one available is too expensive, sharing the baby's parenting with your partner can cut down the nursery hours you need and make the cost manageable. Equally, if there is no nursery place available, you may be happy to settle for a childminder whom you really like provided there are two of you, each with enough flexibility at work that you can cover for each other and the caregiver when she is ill or plans go awry.

The kind of job you mean to take is also crucial, especially its hours. If you are only going to work part-time or half the week, at least to begin with, your child's basic care and upbringing will remain squarely in your hands. Provided he is safe and contented with his caregiver, it will not greatly matter if he is under-stretched during those periods. On the other hand, if you are going to take on a full-time job, especially one that has no flexibility and may even involve extra hours for travel, your baby will spend more than half his waking hours in childcare and you will have to accept that you are sharing not just his daily care but his upbringing. You need to choose accordingly.

Once you have entered into an arrangement, do think very hard before changing it if your baby is happy and doing well. It may be very irritating to be scolded when the train makes you late picking your child up from nursery but if the child loves the nursery you had better find new travel arrangements so you can love it too. And while it may be infuriating to come home from work to a messy house when you're paying high wages, if your child is cheerfully chortling having clearly had a good day, you may need new plans for the housework rather than a new nanny.

You will be doing well if you can find and settle into an arrangement that is right for your child and tolerable for you. However, with a little luck, and the help of *Choosing Childcare*, it may be possible to find a child-carer and setting that are perfect in all respects.

Penelope Leach, Lewes, 2016

Chapter 1

Returning to work or study

Weighing up your work-life balance and childcare choices as your return to work or college approaches

Thinking about childcare for the first time is a big and often daunting step. You've just got used to your new life as a parent, and now you have to make another huge leap to being a working parent. No matter how career-focused you are, and no matter how old your little one is, the prospect of entrusting someone else with care of your precious baby or child is likely to make you feel a little anxious. The range of childcare options on offer may seem confusing too.

Your priority will be for your child to be well looked after, safe and happy, in a setting where they can learn and have fun. The good news is that this could apply to any kind of childcare – nursery, childminder, nanny or grandparents. Most experts agree that it's the quality, not the type, of childcare that matters most, and that the care-giver is far more important than the setting and facilities – especially for babies and toddlers.

There's no 'one-size-fits-all' childcare solution. All types have advantages and disadvantages, and what's perfect for one family may not be right at all for another. It may be helpful to get opinions from friends, family, colleagues, neighbours and online forums, but don't feel pressured by them. Your child, work situation and family set-up are all unique, and you know them best.

Similarly, inspection reports and references provide useful information, but it's also important to trust your feelings and gut instincts. You will be better able to focus on your job or studies if you are confident your child is being well cared for.

Many families use a patchwork of care – for example, mum one day, dad another, grandparents another, and nursery for the remaining two. Bear in mind, too, that your family's childcare needs may change over time, perhaps because you have a new baby, new job, new home, or simply because your child is growing up. It's very common to use two or three different childcare providers before your child reaches school age.

Whichever form of childcare you choose, there will be numerous benefits for you and your family. For you it's a chance to earn some money or perhaps to learn new skills, progress in your career, and regain some independence. At the same time your child will form valuable new relationships, learn new things and benefit from opportunities that may not be available at home with mum or dad. You and your child may also find that you appreciate your time together more when you start to spend some of it apart.

Things to think about

It's best to start with an open mind and not rule out any options unless you have to. Before you begin your childcare search, you might find it helpful to think about the following questions:

Your child's needs

- What's your child's personality type? Sociable, outgoing, enjoys lots of stimulation? Outdoorsy and adventurous? Or calm, shy, home-loving?
- Does your child have any additional needs – medical, physical, behavioural or dietary?
- Are there cultural or religious considerations that are important to you, for example regarding language, food or religious observance?
- Do you have strong views about, for example, behaviour management, your child's diet, the amount of television they watch, or the amount of time they spend outdoors?
- What will be your child's next steps developmentally when you return to work or study (weaning, crawling, walking, talking, potty training, etc) and how will your childcarer support these?

Practical considerations

- Do you and your partner (if you have one) work normal office hours ?
- Are your working hours predictable, or are you often asked to work (or work longer hours) at short notice?
- Would you prefer childcare in, or close to, your home or nearer to work?
- How will you fit mealtimes, childcare pick-ups and drop-offs, housework and so on around your working day?
- What will happen if your child or your regular childcare provider is ill, if your childcarer is unavailable, or in an emergency situation? (Can you or another family member ever leave work early, swap working days or work from home?)
- Is there plenty of childcare provision in your local area, or are your choices limited?
- How much can you afford to pay? (Find more information about paying for childcare, including help that may be available to you, in chapter 9.)

There are no right or wrong answers to any of these questions, but your responses should help you to define your family's requirements and your own personal views on childcare. You'll probably find that there are some areas you're quite flexible about, while others are non-negotiable. Make a note of the issues that matter to you most, and be sure to cover them when you interview any prospective childcarer.

Where to start your search

You'll probably want to find out what sorts of childcare friends, colleagues and neighbours are using, and whether anyone has any recommendations. Your local Family Information Service (FIS) is another good starting point, as they'll have details of all the registered childcare providers in your area.

You can find the Family Information Service for your area via: **www.familyandchildcaretrust.org/findyourfis**

There are also commercial websites to help you find the right childcare provider, such as: **www.childcare.co.uk**

But will a nursery, registered childminder, nanny, au pair or relatives provide the best sort of childcare for your family? The remaining chapters of this book will help you make up your mind.

When to start your search

It's sensible to start thinking about childcare as early as possible. Some providers get booked up many months in advance, and your colleagues may be a useful source of information before you start maternity or paternity leave. That said, when you're pregnant or in the bewildering newborn days, it's impossible to imagine how you will feel about returning to work and leaving your baby with someone else once he or she is a few months old.

If you know that the childcarer you have in mind is particularly sought-after, you might want to approach them when (or even before) your baby is born. You may be able to register your interest or put your child's name on their waiting list (often for a fee), and then sort out the precise days and hours of care you need at a later date.

Generally, though, it's fine to start looking in earnest once you have a clear idea of when you will be returning to your job or studies and what you and your partner's working pattern will be. Ideally, this should be three to six months before you want the childcare arrangement to start. Don't panic if you have less time than this though, as childcare providers sometimes have vacancies at short notice, and there may be newly registered providers with places.

There are certain times of year when childcarers are more likely to have vacancies – notably September, when a new cohort of children starts primary school, and also after the Christmas and Easter holidays, when some children start preschool.

How you might feel

It's very normal to have mixed emotions about the prospect of returning to work and leaving your little one in childcare. On the one hand, you may be looking forward to escaping the drudgery of caring for a small child – at least for some of the time! You may relish the prospect of having a status that's something other than 'mother' (or 'father'), using your professional skills and knowledge again, mixing with colleagues and clients, and of course returning to earning.

People with young children often describe going to work as a 'relief' and a 'sanity-saver'. Many feel that being a working parent makes them a better parent. When you can't be with your child all the time, the time you do spend with them becomes more precious. You may also feel that your child will benefit from childcare – whichever sort you choose – and all the new experiences, opportunities and friendships it will bring.

On the other hand, you will almost certainly feel sadness at the prospect of being apart from your child, no longer able to share in every moment of their growing up. You may feel jealous of others whose lives seem easier and less complicated than yours , or of the carer who will be with your child while you're working. You will probably also worry, both about your little one's safety and wellbeing when you're not there, and about the long-term impact of your work and childcare choices.

As your return to work nears, feelings of self-doubt can creep in: Am I doing the right thing? How will we all cope? What will my family and friends think? These anxieties are an inevitable part of being a parent. Someone who has chosen not to return to work will probably be asking themselves exactly the same questions.

However you are feeling, rest assured that you're not the only one. Millions of parents before you have dealt with these conflicting emotions and the complexities of juggling work and family life, and have come through it all fine. By making an informed choice about childcare, you can be confident you are doing the best for your family in your particular circumstances, which should help to allay the guilt and anxiety a little – if never completely!

What parents say...

It's important to consider the practicalities of your arrangement, as well choosing the right environment for your children. How easy will it be to get there in the rush hour? What's the parking like? What happens if you get delayed? What are the arrangements for meal-times? Are childcare vouchers and early years entitlement accepted? What happens if your child or childcarer are poorly?'
– *Julie, civil servant and mother of two*

Trust your instincts and try to get a sense of the atmosphere of the place you are visiting. Take time to watch and take in what is happening. Observe how the children are behaving towards the carers and vice versa. Is there laughter and affection?'
– *Denise, employee relations consultant and mother of two*

Listen to others' opinions, of course, but remember that most parents' experiences of childcare are limited and they will tend to be loyal to their chosen carer and defend their own choices. It's good to do your own independent research too.'
– *Beth, journalist and mother of two*

You only know which nursery or childminder you will like after you've visited them. It's a personal thing. I thought I wanted a Montessori nursery but didn't get a good vibe from two I visited. Tried several others too, but the minute I walked into the one I even-tually chose I knew it felt right. Now I'm a childminder and I know the same holds true for people who visit me.'
– *Ally, registered childminder and mother of three*

Childcare at a glance

Type of childcare:	Daycare nursery	Registered childminder
Where is the care?	Centre-based.	In the childminder's home.
Typical opening hours?	Five days a week, up to 51 weeks a year, opening at 7am or 8am and closing sometime between 6pm and 7.30pm.	Five days a week, 47 or 48 weeks a year, from around 8am until 6pm is typical, but many childminders adapt their hours to suit parents' needs.
Will they care for children in the evenings, overnight or at weekends?	Not normally.	Some childminders are happy to care for children outside of standard office hours.
Is the care registered and inspected? *	Yes, by Ofsted in England and equivalent bodies in other parts of the UK.	Yes, by Ofsted in England and equivalent bodies in other parts of the UK.
Do they have an enhanced Disclosure and Barring Service check, and training in first aid for children? *	Yes, all nursery staff should have an enhanced DBS check, and at least one should have first aid training.	Yes.
Can I use childcare vouchers, the childcare element of tax credits, or the tax-free childcare scheme?	Yes.	Yes, usually.

* This information covers England only. Rules and regulations may vary in other parts of the UK.

Nanny	Au pair	Grandparents/ family
In your home.	In your home.	Either in your home or the grandparents' home.
A live-out nanny will normally care for children for 10 to 11 hours each weekday, a live-in nanny for around 12 hours a day, for 47 or 48 weeks a year.	Usually up to five hours a day, five days a week, plus two evenings' babysitting.	As negotiated between the parents and grandparents.
Two evenings' babysitting each week is usual. Other hours by negotiation.	Normally two evenings' babysitting.	Very often.
Registration is voluntary. Currently around two-thirds of nannies are registered.	Very rarely.	No (unless the grandparent is also a registered childminder offering childcare to other families).
Yes, if the nanny is registered with Ofsted or their agency requires these.	The au pair should have a police check from their home country, and you may want to arrange first aid training.	Probably not, unless you choose to arrange them.
Only if your nanny is registered.	Not usually, unless your au pair can meet all the requirements of Ofsted registration.	No (unless the grandparent is a registered childminder).

Childcare at a glance Continued

Type of childcare:	Daycare nursery	Registered childminder
What childcare training is required? * (See page 182 for more information about childcare qualifications.)	All managers and supervisors must have at least a level 3 childcare qualification, and at least half of other staff should be qualified to a minimum of level 2.	Introductory childminding training covering children's welfare, safeguarding, development and learning. Many childminders have additional childcare qualifications.
How old are the children cared for?	Normally three months until school age.	Any age, from birth to teens.
What is the ratio of adults to children? *	One adult for every three babies aged under 2; one adult for every four toddlers aged 2-3, one adult for every eight children aged 3+.	Normally registered to care for three pre-school children, including one under 12 months, and a further three schoolchildren up to age 8.
What is the carer's employment status?	Employed by the nursery, or nursery chain, they work for.	Self-employed.
How much will I pay?	Around £3.75 – £7 per hour per child, depending on where you live and what's included in the service (meals, nappies, etc).	Around £3.50 – £6.50 per hour per child, depending on where you live and what's included in the service (meals, nappies, etc).

* This information covers England only. Rules and regulations may vary in other parts of the UK.

Nanny	Au pair	Grandparents/ family
No training is required by law. Many agencies like nannies to have a level 3 childcare qualification, and introductory training is required for the nanny to be registered.	Usually none.	None – but most grandparents have plenty of experience with young children!
Any age, from birth to teens.	Sole care of children under 2 not permitted; sole care of under-4s not advised.	Any age, from birth to teens.
No legal requirements.	No legal requirements.	No legal requirements.
Usually employed by the parents they work for.	Considered to be living as a member of the family; not classed as an employee.	May be an employee of the parents if they receive a wage for the childcare.
£20,000 to £40,000 a year (plus expenses, fees and employer's NI) for a full-time nanny, depending on the area and whether they live with you.	£70 – £85 a week for an au pair. Up to £110 a week for an au pair plus (+ board and expenses).	Many don't charge at all; others may charge a similar amount to a local childminder or nursery.

Will childcare be good for my child?

Every parent wants what's best for their child, but evidence around whether childcare is 'good' for children is often contradictory. Every few months a new study hits the headlines, claiming that spending time in non-parental care helps prepare children for school, or raises their stress levels, or gives them better social skills, or makes them more aggressive and disruptive, and so on, and so on.

The stories about the positive impact of childcare are reassuring, and those about possible harmful effects make parents feel understandably anxious. It's always worth reading beyond the headlines to understand whether the research is actually relevant to you and your child.

Studies carried out overseas may not reflect children's experiences in the UK, as childcare funding, carers' training, regulations, adult:child ratios, and parental leave arrangements vary enormously around the world. Studies that ignore some types of care give an incomplete picture. Journalists love to use emotive language, but 'double the risk' of something, may just mean an increase from 0.1 to 0.2 per cent. Bear in mind, too, that some studies are carried out by researchers seeking self-publicity or working for a commercial organisation with an ulterior motive.

Mass use of paid childcare is still a fairly recent phenomenon, and one seen in relatively few cultures around the world, so we are still learning about its long-term impact. There are, however, a few points that childcare researchers generally agree on:

- A child's family background and home environment influence their intellectual and social development far more than any childcare, even for those whose parents work full time. Warm and loving family relationships and attentive parents are beneficial; an unstable and deprived home-life is not. Simple activities with mum or dad, such as reading stories, singing songs and rhymes, painting and drawing, playing letter and number games, going on outings and playing with friends, will help to give your child a good start in life.
- There is good and bad in all kinds of childcare, including parental

care. What matters most is not the type of care, but its quality.

- Spending time in group daycare seems to have a slightly beneficial impact on very young children's language and social skills and cognitive development by the time they reach school age. It also seems to have a slightly negative impact on their behaviour and emotional development, particularly if children are in centre-based daycare from a very young age. Positive effects are seen equally in children in part-time and full-time childcare. Negative effects tend to be more pronounced in those who spend a lot of time in daycare (over 30 or 35 hours a week, according to some studies).

- High quality childcare and early education are certainly good for children over the age of three, helping to develop social, communication and academic skills, and eventually easing the transition to school.

- Quality childcare is also undoubtedly beneficial to young children of all ages who have deprived or troubled home lives.

- Several international studies have found that babies and children in group childcare experience raised levels of cortisol (often called the 'stress hormone'), and different patterns of cortisol production, compared with their counterparts cared for by parents at home. The effect seems to be most pronounced for very young children who spend long periods in large, busy group settings that provide poor quality care. Some experts have expressed concern about the effect this might have on youngsters' behaviour and brain development; others argue that it's a normal response and may promote children's resilience in the long term. The truth is that there is much we still don't understand and more research is needed.

- When mothers want to work, and have access to reliable, affordable, good quality childcare to enable them to do so, they benefit financially, socially and psychologically – which advantages their children too.

If you're interested in finding out more about the impact of childcare on young children's development, you might want to read:

Child Care Today: What we know and what we need to know
by Dr Penelope Leach (Polity Press, 2009)

What is quality childcare?

We all want the childcare we choose for our children to be good quality, but what does that actually mean? Here are some measures of quality to look out for when you're researching your childcare options and speaking to providers.

Ofsted inspection reports and gradings – These give useful information about nurseries and childminders (and some others types of registered care) in England, including their workplace, working practices and how well they are delivering the Early Years Foundation Stage (see page 187). Bear in mind, however, that they only give a snapshot view of a setting and may be several years out-of-date. Although a 'good' or 'outstanding' grading may be an indicator of high quality care, you'll want to visit the setting and speak to parents who use it to make up your own mind. (NB Other regulatory bodies and childcare standards operate in other parts of the UK – see page 51.)

Quality improvement and quality assurance schemes – Often run by local authorities or childcare organisations, quality improvement or assurance schemes encourage childcare professionals to work to higher standards while enjoying additional mentoring and support. Examples of nationwide schemes include PACEY's Children Come First Childminding Networks and the National Day Nurseries Association's e-Quality Counts for nurseries.

Qualifications, training and experience – Studies suggest that better qualified childcarers deliver better quality childcare, so ask carers about their past training and future plans for professional development. In nurseries, having a qualified teacher or graduate on the leadership team has been shown to enhance the quality of care too.

Good adult:child ratios – All children, but especially babies and toddlers, do best in childcare when they have plenty of focused attention and affection. Choose a set-up where your child's carer is readily available to meet their needs.

Stability and consistency – Babies and toddlers in particular benefit from being able to form a stable and lasting relationship with their childcarer, so enquire about a nursery's staff turnover or an individual carer's future plans. Good pay rates and working conditions generally enhance staff retention and the quality of care.

Efficient management – Whether the care you choose is home-based or centre-based, it will be of higher quality if the environment is well organised and the days planned and structured.

Health and safety – A good childcare environment is one that's safe and hygienic, with effective measures for minimising accidents and controlling the spread of illnesses.

Lots of learning – With plenty of age-appropriate toys, books, equipment, activities and outings, quality childcare will give your little one a wide range of learning opportunities.

Good food – In a quality childcare set-up, meals and snacks will be nutritious, and mealtimes enjoyable social occasions.

Positive interactions – Take time to listen as well as look. In a high quality childcare environment you'll hear plenty of praise, encouragement, co-operation and laughter, and minimal squabbling, shouting and scolding.

Partners in care – Good quality childcare is a two-way partnership between parent and carer. Your childcarer should consult you on, involve you in, and inform you about, all aspects of your child's care.

Different ages, different needs

When deciding what sort of childcare will be best for your family, it's vital to take your child's needs into account as well as your own.

Studies have repeatedly shown that for babies and young toddlers, being able to form a secure attachment to their childcarer is the most important consideration. At this age, finding a childcare arrangement in which your baby can develop a close relationship with an attentive, responsive carer should be your priority.

As toddlers become children, other aspects of their childcare become more significant. Although a strong relationship with their childcarer is still important, you'll also want to look for opportunities for your little one to play, learn and mix with their peers.

Whether a particular childcare setting is 'good' for a particular child depends on a number of factors. As well as age, there's your child's personality type, their individual needs, the amount of time they will spend there, and even your own attitude as a parent.

Your rights as a working parent

Before you can choose a childcare provider, you need to have some idea of how much childcare you'll require and when you want the arrangement to start. Think about how much time you want to spend off work with your new baby and how you're going to manage your finances with an extra mouth to feed and (probably) a reduced household income. Discuss the options with your partner (if you have one) and, if you're employed, read your company's policies on parental leave and pay. If you're unclear about anything, check with your Personnel department or contact one of the organisations mentioned in this chapter.

Maternity Leave

With very few exceptions, women who are employed and pregnant have the right to take up to 52 weeks of Statutory Maternity Leave, made up of 26 weeks' Ordinary Maternity Leave and 26 weeks' Additional Maternity Leave. You can choose to start this at any time during the eleven weeks before your baby is due. If you've been with the same employer for at least 26 weeks by the time of the fifteenth week before your due date and you pay National Insurance, you are entitled to Statutory Maternity Pay. For the first six weeks, this will be 90 per cent of your average weekly pre-tax earnings, and for a further 33 weeks it's £139.58 (in 2016/17) or 90 per cent of your average weekly earnings – whichever is lower.

While you're on maternity leave, you may work up to ten 'keeping in touch' (KIT) days paid at your usual rate. These are optional, taken only if you and your employer both agree to them

Many organisations offer contractual maternity pay which may be higher, or paid for longer, than the statutory minimums, so check exactly what you're entitled to in your workplace.

Adoption Leave

Adoption Leave regulations are very similar to those for Maternity Leave. If you're part of a couple adopting jointly, you can choose which partner takes Adoption Leave.

Shared Parental Leave

Shared Parental Leave and Pay were introduced in April 2015 to give parents more flexibility in deciding how to care for their child in the first year following birth or adoption. You and your partner can choose to have up to 50 weeks of Shared Parental Leave (after two weeks of Compulsory Maternity Leave) to divide between yourselves in whatever way suits you best. You may decide that you both want to take alternating periods of leave, you'd like to take leave together, or you'd prefer to take the leave in up to three separate blocks.

To qualify for Shared Parental Leave, you must have worked for your employer for at least 26 weeks by the time of the fifteenth week before your estimated due date or adoption placement. Your partner must have worked for at least 26 weeks (not necessarily consecutively), and earned at least £30 a week on average in 13 of these weeks, during the 66 weeks before your baby is due. The rules mean that, although one partner must be employed to qualify for Shared Parental Leave, the other may be either employed, self-employed or an agency worker.

Statutory Shared Parental Pay is £139.58 a week (in 2016/17) or 90 per cent of your average weekly earnings, whichever is lower. As with maternity pay, some companies may operate more generous Shared Parental Leave schemes.

While on Shared Parental Leave, you and your partner may each work up to 20 'Shared Parental Leave in touch' (SPLIT) days, paid at your usual rate. These are optional, if both you and your company agree to them, and may be taken in addition to any KIT days you work while on Maternity or Adoption Leave.

Did you know?
In most jobs, you accrue annual leave while you are on parental leave. For example, if you take 52 weeks' Statutory Maternity Leave, and your normal holiday entitlement is 28 days a year, you can – with your employer's agreement – add those 28 days of paid holiday to the end of your maternity leave, or perhaps use one or two days a week to give yourself a phased return to work. There are some exceptions to this rule however, notably in teaching, where accrued leave is normally offset by school holidays.

Paternity leave
Statutory Paternity Leave is a period of one or two weeks' leave which employed fathers may take within 56 days of their baby's birth. It's paid at the statutory rate – ie £139.58 in 2016/17 – if dads meet the qualifying criteria. Shared Parental Leave (see above) replaced the Additional Paternity Leave scheme in April 2015.

During all types of parental leave, employees have certain rights, including to:

- return to your old job (or, in some circumstances, a similar job with the same or better terms and conditions)
- protected terms and conditions of employment
- accrued annual leave
- pay rises
- redundancy rights.

Unpaid Parental Leave

If you've been with the same employer for at least a year, you may also take up to four weeks' Unpaid Parental Leave each year (unless your employer agrees to more). Each parent can take a maximum of 18 weeks of Unpaid Parental Leave for each of their children before the child's 18th birthday. Some parents take a spell of Unpaid Parental Leave at the end of Maternity, Paternity or Shared Parental Leave if they can afford to. Others save it to use if their child ever has any health problems or needs support settling into a new preschool or school, or if their childcare arrangement runs into difficulties. You must give your employer 21 days' notice that you wish to take Unpaid Parental Leave.

Maternity Allowance

Mothers who are self-employed, or who don't qualify for Statutory Maternity Pay, can normally claim Maternity Allowance of £139.58 in 2016/17 (or 90 per cent of your average weekly earnings if this is lower) for up to 39 weeks.

This is only a brief overview of parental leave and pay. What you're entitled to may depend on the nature of your work, how long you have been in your job, the age of your child, your company's policies and other factors. You'll find much more about your rights at work while pregnant or caring for a young baby at:

www.gov.uk/browse/working/time-off
www.workingfamilies.org.uk
www.maternityaction.org.uk

Advice and guidance on parental leave is also available from Citizens Advice (**www.citizensadvice.org.uk**) and Acas (**www.acas.org.uk**).

What parents say...

My wife had our daughter in May and was off work until the end of October, at which point she returned to work and I took over until the end of April. There were two main reasons why we decided to share the leave. The first was that I was very keen to have the time to get to know our daughter and for her not to see me as the strange man who popped in for 15 minutes before she went to bed. The second was that my wife's career is very important to her – she loves her job and didn't want to be off work for a whole year. Our company (we work for the same one) put no obstacles in our way. Our salaries were also broadly at the same level, so it wasn't something that required serious financial re-jigging. I was a bit worried about three months with no pay at all but, as a colleague pointed out, you don't *do* anything expensive when you have a nine-month-old baby anyway. The six months flew by and I'm really glad that I did it.'
– *Tim, publisher and father of one*

I negotiated with my employer to tag my accrued annual leave and 16 weeks of unpaid parental leave (eight weeks for each of my twins) on to the end of my maternity leave. I did this to maximise time with my young family and put off as long as possible the expense of having two children in childcare.'
– *Sandra, trade union legal officer and mother of two*

I decided to do a phased return to work as I had so enjoyed my time off with my little boy and knew I would find it hard going back. I started off by doing my KIT (keeping in touch) days every week or two when he was ten months old. After my year's maternity leave ended, I worked two days a week for a month and a half. Then I did three days a week for two months, before finally settling into my new working pattern of four days a week. I used the annual leave I had accrued during my year's maternity leave to do this. I'm so glad I did it this way as, although I did find it hard, gradually increasing meant my son and I enjoyed as much time together as possible. As he was also starting at nursery, he was able to get used to the weekly routine gradually too. He absolutely loves nursery now.'

– *Sarah, business analyst and mother of one*

Flexible working

All employees who have been working for their employer for at least 26 weeks now have the right to submit a flexible working request. When you and your partner are thinking about how you're going to juggle your jobs with family life and the logistics of childcare, it's worth considering whether one or both of you working flexibly might help reduce your childcare costs and/or give you more time with your family.

Examples of flexible working include:
- working part time
- working from home
- job-sharing
- working compressed hours (ie full-time hours but over fewer days)
- flexitime (ie full-time hours, but with flexibility over when you start and finish)
- working annualised hours (ie working more hours some weeks and fewer in other weeks, adding up to full-time hours over the course of a year).

To make a flexible working request, you need to write to or email your employer stating how you would like to work flexibly and how this might be dealt with (eg if you are not in the office some days), and when you would like the arrangement to start. Your employer may prefer you to use a standard form for this.

Your employer is legally obliged to consider your request, but has up to three months to do so, so make sure you apply in plenty of time. They may only reject your request if there is a clear business case for doing so, and they must put their explanation in writing.

You're allowed to submit just one flexible working request a year, so make sure it's a good one! Make a strong business case that your employer will find hard to challenge. For example, a job-share partner may bring useful new contacts and expertise to the organisation, doing flexitime may mean you're able to reach new customers who aren't available during standard office hours, or there may be tasks you can do more effectively working from home rather than in a busy office. If you have colleagues, or friends in similar jobs, already working flexibly, ask them what they included in their successful application. You'll also find lots of examples online.

This is just a brief overview of flexible working. Find out more at:
www.gov.uk/flexible-working/overview
www.acas.org.uk/flexibleworking

What parents say...

I've had various working patterns since my sons were born, and now they're both at school I do a three-day week, one day working from home. When I'm at home there are no meetings and fewer phone calls, so I have more time to think and am more focused. I can log on to the office network from my laptop and make phone calls using my company's phone system. It's all about doing the work you need to do in the most productive way. Your employer and colleagues have to make it work as much as you do, keeping you up-to-date and organising meetings for days that you're in the office. Flexible working isn't a one-way street – you have to be accommodating and willing to be flexible yourself too.'
 – *Alison, human resources manager and mother of two*

'Putting the girls in nursery from 8am until 5.30pm five days a week felt like too much time away from home. By working compressed hours and doing a nine-day fortnight each, my husband and I were able to take it in turns to have a whole day with the children every week. When either of us changed jobs we would say at interview that the nine-day fortnight was a condition of our employment and we haven't ever been turned down.'
– *Anouska, healthcare service director and mother of two*

'I had no choice but to go back to work full time, but I changed my working hours so I could drop my daughter at nursery at 8am, get to work for 8.15am and then pick her up at 4.30pm. The earlier pick-up time means we miss the traffic and I get to spend some playtime with her before bedtime. Never feel guilty or bad for asking to change your working hours or days to spend time with your child. Those early years are precious and you never get them back.'
– *Gemma, events organiser and mother of one*

'My husband does the drop-off at childcare before he starts work at 9am. My working day is 7.30am–3.30pm, so I can pick the kids up by 4pm. This works for us as we can share the responsibility of the pick-ups and drop-offs and still each do a full working day. The children's time in childcare resembles a school day and is not overly long.'
– *Minette, compliance manager and mother of two*

'After working full time for one year after maternity leave, I reflected that I was neither being an effective mummy nor headteacher, let alone wife. I made a flexible working request to become co-head-teacher, which my board of governors accepted. We have proven at my school over four and a half years that two heads are better than one! The workload and stress are shared and I am able to achieve a more effective work-life balance.'
– *Claire, headteacher and mother of one*

Chapter 2

Daycare nurseries

Reliable, year-round childcare in a stimulating group setting

Daycare nurseries are the ultimate in reliable, hassle-free childcare, with staffing and opening hours that you and your family can depend on all year round. National standards give you peace-of-mind as a parent, and no other form of childcare will provide your little one with access to so many toys, resources, structured activities and playmates.

What is a daycare nursery?

Daycare nurseries may provide care for as few as 10 children or as many as 100. They're often divided by age group, so babies are looked after in one room, toddlers in another, and preschoolers in another. Mixed-age settings, where, babies, toddlers and preschoolers are cared for together, all or some of the time, are becoming more common though. Typical opening hours are 8am until 6pm every weekday, although some may open from 7am to 7pm or 7.30pm, and a handful offer 'out-of-hours' or overnight care if this suits local parents' work patterns. While many open 50 or 51 weeks a year, some are term-time only or close for a few days at Easter and in the summer as well as Christmas.

Some nurseries are part of big chains – Busy Bees, Bright Horizons, Asquith and KidsUnlimited are among the largest in the UK. Being part of a chain means economies of scale for the nursery when training or recruiting staff, buying equipment and resources, or decorating and furnishing premises. Other nurseries are independent or part of a small group, perhaps able to offer unique facilities and a more personal and flexible service. Some may follow a particular philosophy or approach to early years education – turn to page 190 to find out more.

Some employers, and more commonly colleges and universities, provide nurseries on-site for the children of staff or students. These may be subsidised, giving parents childcare that's particularly convenient and affordable. There are also nurseries run by local authorities, sometimes attached to Sure Start children's centres, which may offer free or subsidised care to children deemed to be 'in need'.

Some nurseries, especially those that are part of big chains, operate from purpose-built premises, while others are in converted houses, schools, offices, shops or churches. Whatever the setting, there should be plenty of space and resources to give children lots of different play and learning opportunities, outdoors as well as indoors.

For many parents, a big attraction of nursery care is that their child will be able to participate in activities that might not be possible at home or with a sole carer – large-scale messy play, parachute games, group art projects or performances, for example. Some nurseries have a packed curriculum, offering children the chance to learn a language, cookery, dance or music. And some hold special events such as sports days, picnics or Christmas festivities, giving parents the chance to get to know one another.

All nurseries in England are registered and inspected by the education inspectorate Ofsted (there are other inspection bodies in other parts of the UK – see page 51). They follow the Early Years Foundation Stage (EYFS) framework (see page 188), to ensure children are kept safe and healthy and to support their learning and development. The law requires nurseries in England to have:

- all managers and supervisors qualified to at least a level 3 (ie A level-standard) in a subject relevant to early years education
- at least 50 per cent of remaining staff with a minimum of a level 2 (ie GCSE A*-C-standard) early years qualification
- at least one staff member who has undertaken child protection training
- at least one staff member with an up-to-date paediatric first aid

certificate on duty whenever children are present.
- anyone who prepares or handles food trained in food hygiene
- all staff cleared through an enhanced check by the Disclosure and Barring Service (DBS, formerly Criminal Records Bureau)
- an identified Special Educational Needs Co-ordinator (Senco).

These are minimum standards. A good nursery should support staff in undertaking additional training and may employ workers whose qualifications exceed these levels. On-the-job training in areas such as speech and language development and behaviour is also provided in many settings. Find out more about qualifications for nursery workers on page 182.

The minimum staffing requirements in any Ofsted-registered nursery are:

Age of child	Adult-child ratio
Under 2	1:3
2-3 years	1:4
3-8 years	1:8

There should be at least two members or staff on duty at all times, no matter how many children are present.

Did you know?

Daycare nurseries are not the same as nursery schools or preschools, which offer early years education (usually term-time only) to three- and four-year-olds – and some two-year-olds who have additional needs or whose families receive certain benefits. Many settings offer a combined daycare and preschool service, however, and once your child becomes eligible for their early education funding entitlement at the age of three (or two) you will be able to use it to help cover the costs of sending them there. Find out more about your options for funded early education on page 160.

What are the advantages of using a daycare nursery?

- **Reliability** – many nurseries are open for at least 50 weeks a year, and if any staff are ill or on holiday it's the nursery's responsibility, not yours, to find a suitable replacement.
- **Stimulation** – plenty of toys, equipment, resources, staff and other youngsters for your child to play with.
- **Safety in numbers** – with at least two staff members on duty at all times, there's no unsupervised care.
- **Peace of mind** – all nurseries are registered and inspected by Ofsted in England (and equivalent bodies in other parts of the UK).
- **Consistency** – your child will have their own 'key person' among the nursery's staff, so you and your little one can bond with an individual carer and benefit from a consistent approach.
- **Education** – your child will probably be able to have their funded early education in the same setting as their childcare if you wish, once they reach the age of three (or two in some cases).
- **Socialisation** – your child will have plenty of opportunity to observe and interact with other children, helping them to learn and develop their social skills before they start school.
- **Financial assistance** – by using registered care, you may be eligible for help with your childcare costs, such as the childcare element of Working Tax Credit, childcare vouchers from your employer, or the tax-free childcare scheme from early 2017. And some employers and education providers have their own workplace nursery (or crèche), which may be subsidised.
- **Nutrition** – up to three meals a day, plus nutritious snacks, may be provided, and nurseries are required to offer children a healthy, balanced diet. All under-fives at nurseries throughout the UK are also entitled to a drink of milk each day, free of charge.
- **Parenting support** – staff may provide advice on child development and support with parenting issues. And some may offer evening babysitting too.

And what are the disadvantages?

- Nursery hours are often inflexible, with financial penalties for lateness.
- Fees are often per session (eg all morning or all afternoon), meaning you may have to pay for hours of childcare you don't need.
- Your child may have less one-to-one adult attention than with home-based forms of childcare.
- Siblings of different ages probably won't be cared for together, and most nurseries have no provision for school-aged children (although a few do now run out-of-school clubs too).
- A nursery may not be able to accommodate irregular or unsocial working hours.
- Some nurseries have a high turnover of staff, employ some inexperienced or unqualified workers, or often use agency cover staff, which could affect the quality and consistency of your child's care.
- Mixing with so many other children so young may mean your child contracts more illnesses than they would in home-based childcare.

Did you know?

There is some evidence that young children in nurseries are ill more often – but they may have stronger immune systems by the time they reach school age as a result.

A Canadian study published in 2010 and an Australian one in 2011 found that babies and young toddlers who attended large group daycare settings were more likely to pick up respiratory and ear infections than their peers who were cared for at home or in small group settings. By the time they reached school age, however, the nursery children were less likely to suffer from these illnesses than their classmates. It seems their exposure at a young age provided some immunity as they got older.

How much will I pay?

The Family and Childcare Trust's 2016 survey of childcare charges showed nurseries in Britain typically charging around £110 to £115 for 25 hours' care.

Costs varied depending on the location and the age of the child, with parents of over-twos in Yorkshire and Humberside having the least expensive nursery care costs, averaging £93.60 for 25 hours (£3.74 an hour), while those with babies aged under two in London paid £158.73 (£6.35 an hour).

How can I find a good nursery?

Word-of-mouth – As with all forms of childcare, word-of-mouth is a good starting point. Find out which nurseries friends, colleagues and neighbours use, what they like about them and what they're not so keen on. You could also try asking at local parenting groups or on online forums.

In person – If there's a particular nursery you're interested in – either because it's been recommended to you, you've seen it advertising vacancies, or it's conveniently close to home or work – you might want to knock on the door as you're passing. Not all nurseries will be able to show you around with no notice (remember they have ratios to maintain, a busy routine to stick to and child protection issues to consider), but if the staff are friendly and helpful and the babies and children seem engaged and content, these are signs that it's a good setting.

Ofsted – All daycare nurseries in England are registered and inspected by Ofsted. Each inspection report gives an overall grading – **Outstanding, Good, Requires Improvement** or **Inadequate** – as well as details about the setting and the quality of care provided, including any areas for improvement. You can search for a nursery by name or postcode at: **www.ofsted.gov.uk/inspection-reports/find-inspection-report**

Childcare fairs – Some nurseries may promote their services at childcare fairs, perhaps organised by your local children's centre or voluntary groups such as your local branch of the National Childbirth Trust.

Online – Most nurseries have their own website these days. Some are very basic, but others provide a huge amount of information, such as prospectuses, policies, timetables and menus.

You can also get information about nurseries in your area from your local authority's Family Information Service (FIS), whose contact details are available from:
www.familyandchildcaretrust.org/ findyourfis
Alternatively, try the National Day Nurseries Association:
www.ndna.org.uk/parents
or commercial websites such as:
www.daynurseries.co.uk
www.childcare.co.uk/find/nurseries
www.netmums.com/local-to-you/childcare

Visiting a nursery

Start by contacting the nurseries you're most interested in to see if they are able to accommodate your child for the hours and days you need. If they are, make an appointment to visit.

You'll probably want take your child with you so that you can see how he or she responds to the setting and is welcomed by the staff and other children. You may also want to take your partner or another family member for a second opinion.

When you visit a nursery, imagine you are your child. Is this somewhere that you would want to spend your days and would feel safe and content without mum and dad? Ideally you're looking for a setting where you and your child feel comfortable and at ease, and which seems to be well managed and efficiently run.

You'll start to form an opinion about the nursery before you've even set foot inside. Staff who seem friendly and professional on the phone, and well-maintained, child-focused premises help to give a good first impression.

Other things to look out for on your first visit include:
- a friendly, welcoming atmosphere
- bright, stimulating surroundings, decorated with children's art-work, photos and posters
- a knowledgable, organised and professional manager
- enthusiastic and caring staff who talk confidently about what they and the children are doing, and why
- children who seem content, settled and engaged
- a wide range of play and learning opportunities, including both adult-led and child-led activities and safe outdoor play
- a well-equipped environment, with plenty of good quality toys, books and play equipment
- plenty of space for children to crawl, toddle and run
- an environment that's not too noisy and overwhelming (is there some quiet space?)
- attention to safety and hygiene throughout, including in the kitchen, dining area, toilets and nap areas
- registration documents, food hygiene certificates and insurance certificates clearly on display
- convenient and secure drop-off and pick-up procedures.

Questions you might want to ask
About your childcare needs...
- I'm looking for childcare for (hours/days) from (start date). Can you accommodate this?
- Do you have experience of looking after...? (eg a gluten-intolerant child, a toddler with Down's syndrome, a baby who has washable nappies, or whatever your needs may be)

About the nursery...
- Tell me a bit about the nursery. How long has it been established and who owns it?
- How many children are currently on your books? How are they divided within the premises, and what's the maximum number you can take in each age group?
- Does the nursery have any quality standards or professional awards?
- Does it belong to any professional bodies? (eg the National Day Nurseries Association)

About the staff...
- How many staff do you have? (full-time and part-time)
- What proportion of staff are qualified? What sort of qualifications do they have, and what training and staff development opportunities are available?
- What has your staff turnover been during the past two or three years?
- How do you think your staff's pay and conditions compare with those in other local nurseries? (Attractive pay rates and employment policies help to recruit and keep good staff.)
- What adult:child ratios do you have for different age groups of children? How do you ensure these are maintained during lunch and break times?
- How do you cover short-notice absences? (Do you have your own back-up staff or use agency workers?)
- How does your 'key person' system operate? Would the key person play an active role in caring for my child day-to-day? What happens when a child's key person is absent?
- Can I meet the staff responsible for the room/section my child would be in?

About the nursery routine...
- Tell me about a typical day/week at the nursery. What is the balance

of adult-led and child-initiated activities?
- What arrangements do you have for nap times? (Are there set nap times, or are they child-led?)
- How often are nappies changed? Are older children taken to the toilet at certain times?
- Is outdoor play freely available, or is it at set times?
- Do children of different ages have opportunities to mix?
- Do you take the children on any outings, either regular trips or special excursions?
- What festivals and special events do you celebrate? Are there opportunities for parents and families to get involved?
- What rules do you have for children, and how do you manage their behaviour?

About meals and snacks...
- What times are meals and snacks? What happens if children are asleep, or if they get hungry or thirsty outside these times?
- Do you provide meals and snacks, or do parents have to supply these?
- If meals are provided, are they freshly prepared on site or from an outside caterer? Can you show me a week's menu?
- What is your Food Standards Agency rating?

About health and safety...
- How do you aim to ensure children's safety inside and out?
- How do you ensure children's safety at drop-off and collection times?
- What measures do you take to protect against the spread of infectious diseases?
- What plans do you have for emergency situations? What sort of emergencies have you had to deal with in the past?
- Under what circumstances would you call a parent to collect their child?

About records and reports...
- What sorts of records do you keep?
- What sorts of policies do you have, and how do you make these available to parents?
- How do you like to exchange information with parents?
- Could I see an example of your parents' contract?
- What is your Ofsted registration number (or equivalent outside England)?
- What is your current inspection grading, and do you think their report is a fair assessment of your service? What guidance were you given for improvement, and how are you implementing this?
- Do you have any written references from parents and are there any parents I could contact for a reference?

About financial matters...
- What is your charge per session, day or week? And do your fees cover meals, snacks, drinks, baby milk, outings, nappies and wipes?
- Do you accept childcare vouchers?
- Do you offer funded early education?
- Do you charge a deposit or retainer fee?
- Do you offer a discount for siblings?
- Do you charge for bank holidays?
- Do you implement price rises regularly or on an ad hoc basis?
- What fees are payable when children are on holiday or unwell?
- What is your notice period if I want to withdraw my child or change their hours?
- Is it ever possible to reschedule missed sessions?

About practical issues...
- How do you like to manage a settling-in or trial period? Is there a charge for this?
- It there any clothing or equipment that parents are expected to supply? (For example, sun hats, wellies, slippers, waterproofs.)

– How do you like to exchange information with parents?

And finally…
– Is there anything else you want to mention that I haven't covered?

Securing a nursery place

Once you've found a nursery that meets your needs and those of your child, the next step is to reserve a place. Most nurseries charge a registration fee or deposit when you put your child's name down, and some charge a retainer fee (a regular payment lower than the full fee) if they're keeping a place open for your child that could be filled sooner by another child. Make sure you understand how much you'll be paying and what will happen if your childcare plans change. Many nurseries will refund your deposit by taking it off your final bill when your child eventually leaves their care, but if you aren't able to use the nursery place as planned you probably won't get your money back. Registration and retainer fees are usually not refundable under any circumstances.

Most nurseries have their own standard contract that they ask all parents to sign. Nursery contracts vary enormously, but there will typically be clauses covering:
– names and details of the child, nursery and parents (or guardians), including parents' work and mobile phone numbers
– start date
– days and hours of care required
– nursery opening days and hours (including any regular closures at Christmas or during summer holidays)
– fees and charges (including penalties for collecting your child late; arrangements for bank holidays; any sibling discount offered; whether meals, snacks, outings, baby milk, etc, are covered by the standard fee or paid for separately)
– payment details (including payment dates and methods and procedures for fee reviews)

- arrangements for a settling-in period, including charges and notice
- the notice period required by either party to change or terminate the care arrangement
- arrangements when your child is ill or on holiday, and when the nursery has to close unexpectedly (such as heavy snow or flooding)
- parents' obligations, including behaviour that might result in the termination of the contract.

You will probably also be asked to confirm that you understand and agree with the nursery's policies on matters such as administering medicine, seeking emergency medical treatment, taking children on outings, photographing children, applying suncream, making complaints, child protection, and more. These may be included as part of the contract, or presented as policy documents that you sign separately. Many nurseries will also ask you to provide proof of your address and of your child's identity.

It's good practice for a member of staff to go through the clauses in the contract with you before asking you to sign. Never sign a childcare contract without reading it first. Ask questions about anything you're unsure of, take it away to read and discuss with your partner if you need to, and if there are any clauses you're unhappy with ask if they're negotiable.

Once the contract has been signed and dated by you the parent (ideally everyone who has parental responsibility for the child should sign) and a senior member of nursery staff, it becomes legally binding and you should be given a copy to keep. If your situation changes, for example you move house or need different hours of care, the nursery should amend the contract or draw up a new one for you both to sign. Agreeing changes only verbally could leave you in a weak position if you ever have any kind of dispute.

If you have any queries about the contract after it's been signed, approach the nursery manager in the first instance. If they can't help, try contacting Citizens Advice, Working Families or the National Day Nurseries Association for advice. Ofsted and other inspection bodies can't help with any matters relating to contracts or finances.

With your contract in place, it's time to think about preparing your child for their time at nursery. Turn to chapter 10, *Making it work*, for ideas.

Further information

The National Day Nurseries Association is a UK-wide charity and membership association for nurseries: **www.ndna.org.uk** 01484 407070.

The information in this chapter refers primarily to nurseries in England. Regulations in other parts of the UK vary as follows:

Wales

Nurseries in Wales must meet the National Minimum Standards for Regulated Child Care: **www.gov.wales** (search for 'child care standards'). The Care and Social Services Inspectorate Wales (CSSIW) inspects nurseries in Wales against these standards. To view an inspection report, visit: **www.cssiw.org.uk** There are no inspection gradings at present, although a 'judgement framework' has been piloted.

The Foundation Phase is the statutory curriculum for children aged three to seven in Wales. For more information visit: **www.gov.wales** (search for 'foundation phase') Nurseries that deliver the Foundation Phase are inspected by the education inspectorate Estyn, and you can search for inspection reports at: **www.estyn.gov.uk**

Scotland

Nurseries in Scotland have to meet the National Care Standards, which cover all early education and childcare provision for children up the age of 16. For more information visit **www.nationalcarestandards.org**

The Care Inspectorate inspects nurseries against the National Care Standards. View inspection reports at **www.careinspectorate.com**

For children aged up to three, nurseries follow the Pre-Birth to Three guidance, and for three-year-olds upwards they follow the Curriculum for Excellence framework. There is also Building the Ambition guidance covering all early learning and childcare. Find out more at: **www.educationscotland.gov.uk**

Northern Ireland

In Northern Ireland, nurseries have to meet the National Minimum Standards for Childminding and Daycare: **www.childcarepartnerships-ni.org**

All must be registered and annually inspected by the Early Years Team in the local Health and Social Care Trust. Nurseries that deliver early years education are inspected by the Education Training Inspectorate and you can search for inspection reports online at: **www.etini.gov.uk**

What parents say...

I chose a nursery because I wanted my daughter to get used to lots of people, as it was just myself and her at home. Also at such a young age (16 months), I didn't feel ready to trust her care to just one person I didn't really know, and I didn't want to work around one person's sick leave or holiday. The first nursery I chose for my daughter had a homely feel and fantastic staff. The second was even better. It had just 24 children and offered activities such as music, French, yoga, creative drawing and dancing. It prepared my daughter for school and helped her become very sociable and confident. Sending her to nursery is the best decision I ever made.'
– Fay, website editor and mother of one

We chose a nursery that's part of a national chain. I like the ethics of the company – they seem to have reasonable staff development, training, and career progression opportunities, and a focus on including male carers too. The care is good, with the days structured and varied, a key person for each child, and freshly made food provided. The activities are wide-ranging and include things that it's not always easy for us to fit in at home, like cooking with the kids or messy art play. There's lots of space for children to play inside and out, and plenty of toys and equipment. The location and hours are convenient for us, especially as it's open all year round.'

– *Jenni, IT analyst and mother of two*

My husband and I opted for daycare nurseries as we preferred the purpose-built set-up. We also needed 100 per cent reliability in our childcare and we wanted to take holiday to look after our kids when we chose to, as opposed to when an individual carer was unavailable. As both our children were shy in their nature, we wanted them to be able to mix confidently with other children and adults. I looked for flexibility – something I have been lucky to find with the two nurseries we have used. Both nurseries also provided good quality food and snacks and did not use "value" brands, which for me is a sign that it's not all about the bottom line but about what's good for the children.'

– *Denise, employee relations manager and mother of two*

I chose a nursery close to my work, as I knew my sister was very happy with the way her children were cared for there. The staff were so welcoming and you could see the children loved every second of their time there. Unfortunately the nursery closed. The chain opened a much larger one, but when we went to look round (twice) I could see my little girl was not happy there, and I wasn't keen on the set-up or the attitude of the staff. So we settled on a small independent nursery. The staff were friendly and put both myself and my daughter at ease. She has grown so much in confidence over the last few months since she started there. She is really happy, talks constantly about her nursery friends and sings at the top of her lungs all the songs she has learnt.'

– *Gemma, events organiser and mother of one*

Chapter 3

Registered childminders

A flexible and personal childcare service in a home-from-home setting

If you like the idea of a 'home-from-home' childcare setting, and a childcarer that you and your little one can form a close bond with, then a registered childminder could be the perfect option for you. A childminder may also be ideal if you need childcare outside of usual working hours, your work pattern is variable, there are no nurseries in your area, or your child has additional needs and would benefit from a more personal level of care.

What is a registered childminder?

Registered childminders usually work in their own home caring for other people's children, sometimes alongside their own children or grandchildren. They are self-employed, and so decide their own working hours, fees and business practices. For example, some offer cooked meals while others prefer parents to provide packed lunches, and while most work weekdays, some look after children at weekends or overnight. Unlike nannies, childminders are responsible for their own tax, National Insurance and insurance policies.

The vast majority of registered childminders are women, and most are mothers themselves. Some work with a co-childminder or assistant, perhaps their spouse, daughter, sister, friend or a student helper. Many belong to a childminding group or network, allowing them to share ideas and resources, provide back-up for sickness and emergencies, undertake training together, and give the children in their care the chance to mix with others of a similar age.

Childminders must be registered and have their working premises inspected by Ofsted or a childminder agency in England (or other relevant bodies in other parts of the UK). In England they are normally allowed to care for up to six children under the age of eight, including their own children or grandchildren. Of these six, only three may be of pre-school age, and normally only one of these can be a baby aged under 12 months (although exceptions may be made, for example for twins). When deciding exactly how many children a childminder can be registered to care for, Ofsted (or any other registering body) will take into account the amount of space in the home, the childminder's experience, any older children in the household, and any co-childminders or helpers.

Childminding is not just daytime babysitting. It's a responsible and demanding job, and registration requirements have become increasingly rigorous in recent years. Anyone wanting to become a childminder in England must first:
- attend an introductory training course covering children's welfare, safeguarding, development and learning
- undertake a certified 12-hour training course in paediatric first aid
- complete a health declaration, checked and signed by their GP, to say they are fit to work with young children
- be cleared by the Disclosure and Barring Service (DBS, formerly the Criminal Records Bureau) – as will all other adults in their household
- have their home inspected and be interviewed by Ofsted or a childminder agency, to ensure they can meet the requirements of the Early Years Foundation Stage (see page 188)
- arrange specialist public liability insurance, and vehicle insurance too if they plan to take childminded children out in their car.

Like all registered childcarers working with under-fives in England, childminders have to follow the Early Years Foundation Stage (EYFS), the framework that guides children's learning until the end of their first year at school (see page 188). They are not allowed smack or use other corporal punishment, and they must ensure children are cared for in a smoke-free environment. They must also have a range of written policies covering issues such as child protection, behaviour management and administering medicines.

Some childminders may also choose to be part of a quality assurance scheme, through which they receive additional training and have regular observations of their childcare practice.

Children cared for by a childminder benefit from real-life learning experiences, such as cooking, gardening and family mealtimes, and trips to the local park, library or shops. Activities may also be more spontaneous and child-led than in larger settings, so your child might be running through the garden sprinkler on a hot day, going on a welly-walk when it's wet, or doing activities inspired by their latest obsession – whether that's dinosaurs, castles or space travel.

The advantages of using a registered childminder?

- **Consistency** – your child will form a stable relationship with a single carer.
- **Home-from-home** – the care is usually in domestic premises, which may help your child to feel at ease.
- **Mixed-age** – your child will be in a small group of children of different ages, similar to a sibling group. Children cared for by child-minders learn from those older and younger than themselves and often form lasting friendships.
- **Family-friendly** – siblings of different ages can be cared for together, including school-aged children after school and in the holidays.
- **Part of the community** – your child will probably have opportuni-ties to get out and about in the local area, to parks, libraries, toddler groups and visitor attractions.
- **Flexibility** – childminders often offer a more personal and adaptable service than other childcare providers. This can be helpful if your working hours are irregular or your child has additional needs. Some childminders offer care outside of the standard working day,

which is ideal if your job involves shifts or unsocial hours.

- **Peace of mind** – childminders are registered and inspected by Ofsted or a childminder agency in England (equivalent bodies elsewhere in the UK).
- **Financial support** – by using registered care, you may be eligible for help with your childcare costs, such as the childcare element of Working Tax Credit, childcare vouchers from your employer, or the tax-free childcare scheme from early 2017.
- **Education** – your childminder may be able to offer the funded early education entitlement, once your child becomes eligible for it at the age of two or three.
- **Nutrition** – up to three meals a day plus snacks may be provided, and childminders are required to offer children a healthy, balanced diet. They may also claim free milk for the children in their care.
- **Parenting support** – as the vast majority of childminders are parents themselves, they may become a valued source of advice and support as your child grows and develops.

And the disadvantages?

- You're usually dependent on just one person for your childcare, so will need back-up if they're ill or away.
- Babies and toddlers may have to fit in with the childminder's routine of school and preschool pick-ups – although these regular outings can be a learning opportunity and a chance for young children to become familiar with establishments they may attend in future.
- Unless your childminder has a partner or assistant, they will be working alone and unsupervised, so you need to trust them absolutely.
- Working in a home environment, childminders are unlikely to offer the space and facilities of a nursery.
- You are not the childminder's employer, so don't have as much control over how your child is cared for as you might with a nanny.

How much will I pay?

According to the Family and Childcare Trust's Annual Childcare Costs Survey 2016, childminders around Britain typically charge around £104 a week for 25 hours' care for a baby or toddler. Costs vary greatly depending on the region and the age of the child, with parents of over-twos in the North West paying on average £88.21 for 25 hours' care (£3.53 an hour), while those with a child aged under two living in London pay £148.12 (£5.92 an hour). In all regions, and for all ages, the 2016 survey showed childminders charging slightly less than local nurseries.

When comparing the rates charged by different childminders and other childcare providers, make sure you're clear exactly what the fee covers. Meals, snacks, drinks, nappies, baby wipes, and outings are some of the things that may or may not be included.

Many childminders charge a non-refundable deposit when you reserve a place for your child, so they are not left out-of-pocket if you change your mind. Some charge a retainer fee (a regular payment lower than their normal fee) if you want them to keep a place available for your child until you are ready to use it, to compensate for not being able to offer the place to another child sooner.

How can I find a good childminder?

Word of mouth Start by asking friends, neighbours and colleagues. See if staff at your local school, preschool or children's centre have any recommendations. Or if you're a member of a local parents' online forum or social networking group, try asking there.

Family Information Service Your local authority's Family Information Service (FIS) has details of every childminder in your area, so you can call them to get details of those closest to you.

Most FISs offer a 'childminder finder' through their website, where you input your postcode and search for the childminders closest to you with vacancies. A childminder's FIS listing will usually give you an idea of the facilities and services they offer, and their personality too. Bear in mind though that some childminders may choose not to have their details online, perhaps for privacy reasons or because they don't currently have any vacancies (but they might have by the time you need childcare). If you live or work close to a county or local authority boundary, you may want to contact more than one FIS to expand your pool of potential childminders. **www.familyandchildcaretrust.org/findyourfis**

Ofsted Just like schools and nurseries, all registered childminders in England have Ofsted reports which can be viewed on the Ofsted website, and are searchable by postcode. The reports give an overall grading – **Outstanding, Good, Requires Improvement** or **Inadequate** – and details about the childminder's premises, working practices and standard of care. Some identify the childminder by name, but most just give a unique reference number (URN), so if you find a report that interests you, you'll need to get in touch with your FIS (see above) to get contact details of the childminder with that number. **www.reports.ofsted.gov.uk**

Childminder agencies Childminder agencies were introduced by the Government in September 2014 as an alternative to Ofsted for register-ing and inspecting childminders in England. If there is an agency in your area it will be able to provide you with details of local childminders. Childminders who are part of an agency don't have an individual Ofsted grading – it is the agency that is inspected and graded by Ofsted. Your Family Information Service (see above) should be able to tell you if there are any childminder agencies in your area.

Childcare fairs Childcare fairs can be a good opportunity to meet several childminders at once, and to compare and contrast them with other local childcare providers. Childcare fairs may be organised by your local children's centre, or by voluntary groups such as your local branch of the National Childbirth Trust.

Advertisements Childminders with vacancies may advertise in local newspapers or on bulletin boards in newsagents and supermarkets.

Online matching services Some childminders advertise their services online through commercial websites such as **www.childcare.co.uk** and **www.ichild.co.uk/directory.**

Making contact

Once you've got details of some childminders that interest you, the next step is to contact them. The best times to call are generally after lunch and before the school run, when younger children will probably be napping, or in the evening when most of their young charges have gone home.

Start by finding out if the childminder has a vacancy for your child for the hours and days that you need and, if so, make an appointment to meet them.

Many childminders are happy for parents to visit during their working hours, but some prefer the initial meeting to be at a time when they won't be distracted by the children in their care. In this case, you'll want to do a follow-up visit so you can see the childminder at work and watch how she or he interacts with your child.

Interviewing a childminder

When you visit the childminder's home, imagine you are your child. Is this somewhere that you would want to spend your days and would feel safe and content without mum and dad? Ideally you're looking for a childminder you instinctively warm to, and who has a good rapport with your child and the others in their care. Observe the other children too – do they seem happy and purposeful? Do they interact well together and make you and your child feel welcome?

Childminders work in all sorts of homes, from modest city-centre flats to huge country houses. Whatever the size and location, look out for:
- a friendly, welcoming atmosphere
- bright, stimulating surroundings, perhaps decorated with children's artwork, photos, posters or mobiles
- a range of play and learning opportunities, including outdoor play

(this may be at a local park or public garden if the childminder has no garden)
- a well-equipped environment, with plenty of good quality toys, books and play equipment
- attention to safety and hygiene throughout, including in the kitchen, dining area, toilets and nap areas
- the childminder's registration documents and insurance certificates clearly on display.

Questions you might want to ask

About your childcare needs...
- I'm looking for childcare for (hours/days) from (start date). Are you available?
- Do you have experience of looking after...? (eg baby twins, a child with cerebral palsy, a child whose first language isn't English, or whatever your needs may be)

About the childminder...
- Tell me a bit about yourself and your family.
- When and why did you decide to become a childminder?
- What do you like best about the job?
- How many other children do you currently care for, and how long have they been with you?
- What training and qualifications do you have?
- Are you part of a quality assurance scheme?
- Are you a member of PACEY? (Or other professional membership organisation?)
- Are you part of a childminding group or network?
- Do you work with any co-childminders or assistants?
- Do you have any pets? (Do the children have contact with them?)
- What are your future plans? (Remain in childminding? Stay in same house? Further training, etc?)

About the childminding routine...
- Tell me a bit about a typical childminding day/week? (Activities? Outings? Playgroups? School/preschool runs?)
- What are your house rules, and how do you manage children's behaviour?
- What arrangements do you have for meals and snacks? And how do you ensure the children in your care have a nutritious, balanced diet?
- Do you take the children out in the car? (What sort of car and car seats do you have?)
- What arrangements do you have for nap times?
- Do the children in your care have contact with any other members of your household or visitors to the home?

About records and reports...
- What sorts of records do you keep?
- Do you have a portfolio of childminding documents and policies I could see?
- How do you like to exchange information with parents?
- What is your Ofsted registration number? (Or equivalent outside England.)
- What is your current inspection grading, and do you think the report is a fair assessment of your service? (NB some childminders in England are part of childminder agencies and may not have had an individual Ofsted inspection)
- What guidance were you given for improvement, and how are you implementing this?
- Do you have any written references from parents, and are there any parents I could contact for a reference?

About financial matters...
- What is your hourly/daily charge? And do your fees cover meals, snacks, drinks, baby milk, outings, nappies and wipes?
- Do you accept childcare vouchers? (If your employer offers them,

or your partner's does.)
- Do you offer funded early education (see page 160)
- Do you charge a deposit or retainer fee?
- Do you offer a discount for siblings?
- Do you charge for bank holidays?

About practical issues...
- How do you like to manage a settling-in or trial period? (Including fees.)
- What arrangements do you have for holidays – yours and ours?
- What arrangements do you have for sickness – yours and children's?
- What plans do you have for emergencies?

And finally...
- Is there anything else you want to mention that I haven't covered?

Securing a place with a registered childminder

Once you've found the right childminder, the next step is to secure a place for your child. Most childminders charge a deposit when you reserve a place, and many charge a retainer fee (a regular payment lower than the full fee) if they're keeping a place open for your child that could be filled sooner by another child.

Make sure you understand how much you'll be paying and what will happen if your childcare plans change. A deposit may be refunded once you start to use the childminding service or when your child leaves the childminder's care, but retainer fees are usually non-refundable.

It's important to agree a written contract that gives details of the childminding arrangement and explains responsibilities and expectations on both sides. The majority of childminders use standard contracts devised by PACEY or childcare insurance specialists Morton Michel, which have been approved by these organisations' solicitors.

Among the clauses you can expect to find in a registered childminding contract are:

- name and contact details of the childminder, and often their registration and insurance details too
- names and details of the child and parents (or guardians), including parents' work and mobile phone numbers
- start date
- days and hours of care required
- any deposit or retainer fee payable
- childminding fees, other charges and payment details
- arrangements for a settling-in period, including charges and notice
- the notice period required by either party to change or terminate the care agreement
- arrangements when the childminder or your family are on holiday, and if the childminder or your child is ill
- parents' obligations, including behaviour that might result in termination of the childminding arrangement
- arrangements for reviewing the contract.

You will probably also be asked to confirm that you understand and agree with the childminder's policies on matters such as administering medicine, seeking emergency medical treatment, taking children on outings, taking children out in the car, photographing children, applying suncream, making complaints, child protection, and more. These will often be presented as policy documents that you sign separately.

It's good practice for the childminder to go through the clauses in the contract with you before asking you to sign, Never sign a childcare contract without reading it first. Ask questions about anything you're unsure of, take it away to read and discuss with your partner if you need to, and if there are any clauses you're unhappy with ask if they're negotiable.

Insist on a written contract even if your childminder is a friend or family member, as it gives both of you protection if the childcare arrangement doesn't work out. If more than one of your children will be going to the

Did you know?

Anyone who is paid (or receives any other reward) to care for a child who is not a relative, outside of the child's own home, for more than three hours continuously must be registered as a childminder. However, this rule does not apply between the 'exempted hours' of 6pm to 2am, which means it's fine for your child to go to a friend or neighbour who isn't a registered childminder for an evening's paid babysitting while you go out, but it's against the law for you to pay the same friend or neighbour to look after the same child for more than three hours while you work during the day!

In 2009, two job-sharing police officers hit the headlines because each was caring for the other's daughter when not on duty. Ofsted argued that this childcare swap constituted a 'reward' for both of the women involved, and that they were therefore flouting the Childcare Act 2006 unless they registered as childminders. After public outcry, the Government intervened and the Education Secretary wrote to the Head of Ofsted to clarify that friends doing childcare swaps shouldn't need to register.

Ofsted's own guidance now states that childcarers do not need to register if they only care for the children of one or more friends in their own home or someone else's home:

- if no money or payment changes hands; (or)
- for three hours or less per day and some payment is made.

For more information about circumstances in which childcare doesn't need to be registered, take a look at the Ofsted factsheet 'Registration not required':
www.gov.uk/government/publications/
factsheet-childcare-registration-not-required

childminder, you should sign a separate contract for each child. Once the contract has been signed and dated by you the parent (ideally everyone who has parental responsibility for the child should sign) and the childminder, it becomes legally binding and you should be given a copy to keep. If your situation changes, for example your child starts school or needs different hours of care, the childminder should amend the contract or draw up a new one for you both to sign. Agreeing changes only verbally could leave you in a weak position if you ever have any kind of dispute.

If you have any queries about the contract after it's been signed, approach the childminder in the first instance, or their network coordinator or agency manager if they have one. If they can't help, try contacting Citizens Advice (**www.citizensadvice.org.uk**), Working Families (**www.workingfamilies.org.uk**) or PACEY (**www.pacey.org.uk**) for advice.Ofsted and other inspection bodies can't help with any matters relating to contracts or finances.

With your contract in place, it's time to think about preparing your child for their time with the childminder. Turn to chapter 10, 'Making it work', for ideas.

Further information

The information in this chapter refers primarily to England. Registration and inspection requirements for childminders in other parts of the UK differ slightly. The regulatory bodies and standards governing childminders around the UK are the same as those listed for nurseries on page 51. In addition, you may find the following organisations helpful:

England and Wales
Professional Association for Childcare and Early Years
www.pacey.org.uk 0300 003 0005

Scotland
Scottish Childminding Association
www.childminding.org 01786 449063

Scottish Family Information Service:
www.scottishfamilies.gov.uk

Northern Ireland
Northern Ireland Childminding Association
www.nicma.org 028 9181 1015
NI Direct
www.nidirect.gov.uk/childminders

What parents say...

⟨ What I like about our childminder is the personal service. She's hugely experienced and has four grown-up children of her own, so she's been a great source of advice when we've been tackling issues such as fussy eating and toilet training. She offered to look after our daughter any time, day or night, when baby two came along. She's very reliable and has always been incredibly accommodating and flexible whenever we've needed to change our hours or swap a day. As she works with assistants, there's always more than one adult caring for the children, which I find reassuring. She offers funded early education, which was a great help in easing our daughter's transition to preschool. I also really like the mixed-age setting. Our little girl loved playing with and learning from the older children when she was younger, and now, aged three, she enjoys helping to welcome new starters. Being part of a childminding 'family' has been hugely beneficial to her, and now to her little brother too.'
– *James, researcher and father of two*

⟨ Having a childminder has been an excellent option now my elder child is at school. It provided him with a wonderful, homely environment as he settled into reception and has enabled my

children to remain together after school, helping my younger child adjust to my return to work. I really value the flexibility my childminder offers. On the odd occasion when my train is delayed I no longer have to worry because I can't get home before the nursery closes, and my daughter is able to attend our preferred preschool because my childminder is happy to drop off and collect her.'
 – *Julie, civil servant and mother of two*

I wanted my children to continue doing the things I was doing with them in a home-from-home environment, such as going to the park, playgroups, even going shopping. My childminder was able to follow each child's routine (as much as possible), which included naps in separate bedrooms. She had a good set-up in her house, with a dedicated room for all the activities and toys, and the food she provided was all home-cooked. What I liked best was the amount of love and attention she gives each of the children she looks after, and all the activities she does with the kids, such as taking them to the seaside or parks for picnics, as well as day-to-day outings such as going to playgroups and doing the school run.'
 – *Kerry, senior hydrologist and mother of two*

My decision to use a childminder was driven partly by cost and partly by my daughter's age. Nurseries in my area are hugely expensive and, as my little girl was still under a year, I personally felt she was too young to be left in a big group with lots of other children. I wanted her to be socialised, but I also wanted her to have plenty of one-to-one adult attention. My childminder was recommended to me by someone I work with. Our first visit was for an hour, and within minutes my daughter was playing happily and interacting with the other little girl there. I had peace-of-mind straight away. My daughter benefits massively from the huge variety of activities and experiences the childminder provides – painting, baking, trips to the library, learning through play, activity days at the softplay centre – far more than she would probably do if she was cared for by me at home! She also has a really close bond with the other, slightly older, girl the childminder cares for, which is lovely. I need a lot of flexibility in my childcare as my working days and hours can change at short notice. My childminder is amazing, allowing me to swap days or do an early drop-off whenever I need to. She's also fantastic with the children – incredibly patient and brilliant with their behaviour.'

– Jo, retail manager and mother of one

'As I work shifts, a childminder was the most flexible option for my needs, especially as weekends are required too. I chose my childminders as my child seemed completely settled as soon as I went to see them and their facilities. My son took to them straight away, they seemed very friendly and approachable and were most accommodating in following his routine, using reusable nappies whilst there, providing overnight stays, offering flexibility for when I finish late and just being all-round generally brilliant! Although they're not far from where I work, they sometimes drop him home or meet me wherever it's convenient. The fees are good too – they only charge for the hours he's there, and I pay a flat rate for overnight care from 7pm–7am. Most important of all, my son loves going there and quite happily stays overnight. I think I'm very lucky!'

– Keren, police officer and mother of one

Chapter 4

Nannies

Flexible childcare in your
own home, tailored to
your personal needs

M any people see nannies as the 'gold standard' in childcare. A nanny looks after your children in your own home, offering care that's convenient, suits your family's needs and gives you plenty of say in how your little ones are cared for. Your nanny will probably take care of some child-related chores and appointments too, freeing up precious non-work hours to enjoy with your children. Of course, this very personal form of childcare comes at a price, but if you have two or more children, or if convenience and control are particularly important to you, then a nanny may be your perfect childcare choice.

What is a nanny?

A nanny is employed by parents to look after their children in the family's home. The nanny normally has sole charge of the children and is expected to take care of every aspect of their wellbeing – from providing fun and educational activities to preparing nutritious meals, and often tidying their rooms and doing their laundry too.

Nannies are not required by law to have any particular qualifications, training or experience. In practice, though, most will have a level 3 child-care qualification (see page 182) or several years' experience caring for children – often both.

There are two types of nanny: live-out and live-in...

Live-out nannies

A live-out or daily nanny lives separately from your family and comes to your house every workday, normally working for 10 or 11 hours a day.

Depending on your working hours and preferences, they may get your children up, dressed and breakfasted in the mornings and/or do their tea, bath and bedtime at the end of the day. They may also do some evening babysitting or weekend childcare, either as part of their contract, or negotiated as an added extra.

Live-in nannies

A live-in or residential nanny has their own room or annex in your family home. They are typically expected to be on duty for around 12 hours a day, and may do some evening and weekend childcare too by prior arrangement. Wages for a live-in nanny are usually significantly lower than for their live-out colleagues (see page 79) as their accommodation and some other living costs are included in their job package. To consider taking on a live-in nanny, you need to have sufficient room in your house and feel comfortable about sharing your home with an employee.

The number of residential nannies has fallen in recent years, as more nannies prefer to live independently and fewer families have the space to accommodate staff. According to the 2015 Nannytax Wages Survey, just 10 per cent of nanny employers have a live-in nanny.

Nanny-shares

Some nannies work as a nanny-share, either dividing their working time between two or more families, or caring for children from two families together. The British Association of Professional Nannies (BAPN) suggests that wages for a nanny-share are around 20 to 25 per cent higher than for a nanny working for just one family, to reflect the challenges of juggling two families' needs. Even so, the arrangement still works out far cheaper for parents than employing a nanny for their sole use. If the nanny is working for both families at the same time, there's the added benefit of the children having a playmate.

It can be difficult, though, to find another family whose working hours, parenting ethos, and children's ages and routines all match yours closely enough to consider using the same nanny. And whenever children from two families are cared for together, one family misses out on the benefits of having care provided in their own home. Although a nanny-share is often suggested on parenting websites and in magazines as an ideal solution to families' childcare needs, in the 2015 Nannytax survey just 4 per cent of UK nannies described themselves as 'working in a nanny-share'.

If you are contemplating a nanny-share, you will need to work out issues such as:

- which family's house the nanny will work from (and whether the other family will contribute to costs such as insurance and wear and tear), or whether the care will be in different houses on different days
- who will be the nanny's employer if children from two families are cared for together (the most usual arrangement is the two sets of parents are being joint employers)
- who will provide food for the nanny and children
- what will happen if any of the children is ill
- what the holiday arrangements will be for all involved
- what will happen if either of the families has another child
- what will happen if one family wants to change or end the arrangement.

There are specialist websites that, for a small fee, help connect families interested in nanny sharing .

Try **www.nannyshare.co.uk** for example.

Did you know?

If a nanny cares for children from three or more families together, she or he is required by law to register as a childminder.

Part-time nannies

It's becoming increasingly common for nannies to work part time, providing care for just a few days a week or only after school. In the 2015 Nannytax Wages Survey, a third of nannies said they were currently working part time.

What are the advantages of employing a nanny?

- **Convenience** – a nanny can get your children through their morning routine, so all you need to worry about is getting yourself ready and off to work. And the nanny can do as much or as little of the children's evening routine as you wish.
- **Control** – no other form of paid childcare gives you so much control over your child's day. A nanny can maintain each child's existing timetable of meals and snacks, naps and activities.
- **Care at home** – your children will be in their home environment and have access to their own toys and other belongings.
- **Family-friendly** – children of different ages can be cared for together, and the nanny will probably be able to do school and pre-school runs for you.
- **Household help** – the nanny will probably carry out some domestic chores for you. These are normally child-related tasks, such as cooking their meals, doing their laundry and tiding their bedrooms and play areas.
- **Organisation** – the nanny can take your children to appointments, classes, parties, playdates and more, and deal with administration and correspondence for all of these.
- **Sickness care** – the nanny will probably be able to care for your children if they are unwell.
- **Additional hours** – the nanny might be prepared to do some evening or weekend babysitting (especially if she or he lives in), and may be able to do overtime if you are delayed getting home.
- **Financial support** – if the nanny is registered, you may be able to get

help with payment, such as the childcare element of Working Tax Credit or Universal Credit, employer-supported childcare vouchers, or the tax-free childcare scheme from early 2017 (see chapter 9).

- **Cost-effective** – as payment is per family, not per child, a nanny may be the cheapest childcare option if you have several children.
- **One-to-one** – the individual care provided by a nanny in your own home should help children feel at ease, and may particularly suit a child who has a chronic medical condition, disability or special educational needs.
- **Care on the move** – a nanny may be able to come on holidays or work trips with you, continuing to provide childcare while you are away from home.

And what are the disadvantages?

- Nannies don't have to be registered or have their working premises inspected, so you will need to carry out checks yourself instead.
- Being the nanny's employer means you are responsible for paying their tax and National Insurance and your own employer's NI contributions. You also have responsibilities regarding the nanny's pension and holiday, sickness, maternity and redundancy rights and pay.
- You are dependent on just one person, so will need back-up care if they are ill, on holiday or take maternity leave.
- The nanny is in sole charge of your children and your home, so you need to have complete trust in them.
- Some nannies have firm ideas about discipline, routine, mealtimes and so on,which may be different from yours.
- Privacy and confidentiality may be issues for you or your nanny.
- You must make sure you have appropriate insurance for yourself as an employer, and for your home and car.
- A nanny is often much more expensive than other forms of childcare, especially if you only have one child.

How much will I pay?

Nannytax, the nanny payroll company, carries out an annual survey of nannies' earnings in the UK. In 2015, the average gross annual salaries for daily nannies were:

Central London – £34,554
Greater London and Home Counties – £31,174
Rest of UK – £25,325

Live-in nannies' average gross earnings in 2015 were:

Central London – £21,604
Greater London and Home Counties – £23,795
Rest of UK – £21,253

Remember that on top of the nanny's salary, if your nanny earns over £155 a week (in 2016/17) you will also have to pay employer's National Insurance contributions. These amount to either 10.4 per cent or 13.8 per cent of the nanny's gross pay, depending on factors such as the nanny's age, pension arrangements and any other jobs they may have NI contributions are also payable on any expenses and perks you give your nanny. Other costs to factor in include:

- day-to-day expenses (a kitty of £5 a day for activities, outings and snacks amounts to over £1,000 a year)
- agency fees, if you find your nanny through an agency (see below)
- payroll company fees (normally £100–£300 a year), if you use them
- petrol, travel tickets or mileage allowance (if your nanny uses their car to drive your children, they can claim 45p per mile from you as expenses)
- the nanny's food and drink during working hours
- additional energy costs and wear and tear on your home
- back-up cover for sickness and holidays.

New 'auto enrolment' pension regulations mean that some time before early 2018 you will become responsible for enrolling your nanny into a workplace pension scheme if she or he is aged between 22 and state retirement age and earns over £10,00 a year. Find out more from: **www. thepensionsregulator.gov.uk**

Be aware that, traditionally, nannies have negotiated net rates of pay (ie their take-home pay). Many agencies and most nannies themselves still discuss pay in net terms, but the actual cost to you is likely to be 30 to 40 per cent higher than this. Make sure you know exactly what you're agreeing to. It's best to specify gross pay in the nanny's contract so that if their tax rate changes, the amount you pay will not.

It may be tempting to pay your nanny in cash to avoid paying tax, but this is illegal and you (not your nanny) will face harsh financial penalties, and possibly criminal prosecution, if found out by HM Revenue and Customs. Paying a nanny in cash also cheats them of contributions towards their state pension and other benefits.

Nanny fees are not tax-deductible – so there's no need to mention them when completing a self-assessment tax form. It's no longer possible to pay less tax by setting your nanny up as a company. And your nanny can't be self-employed unless they choose their working hours and days and have some control over their duties and rate of pay.

Voluntary registration for nannies

Although nannies are not required by law to be registered, they can register voluntarily as a 'home childcarer' with Ofsted in England (and other bodies in other parts of the UK). If your nanny is registered, you will be able to use tax-free childcare vouchers from your employer as payment towards their fees, if your employer offers these. You can also claim the childcare element of Working Tax Credit or Universal Credit, if you are eligible for these benefits. And you can take advantage of the tax-free childcare scheme from early 2017. (See chapter 9 for more information on all of these.)

Voluntary registration with Ofsted takes up to 12 weeks and costs £105 a year (in 2016). To apply, a nanny must have:
– a recognised childcare qualification (see page 182)
– basic training in first aid for children, completed within the last three years (this costs around £120)

- an enhanced check from the Disclosure and Barring Service within the last three years, to show there is nothing in their background that may make them unsuitable to work with children. This can be done through **www.ofsteddbsapplication.co.uk** for £44 + fees, or through a most nanny agencies for around £60–£80. You can check a nanny's DBS status via **www.gov.uk/dbs-update-service**.
- public liability insurance, in case a child in their care suffers any injury or causes any damage while the nanny is on duty (this costs £60 to £90 a year).

Your nanny may already be registered (the 2015 Nannytax survey showed that almost two-thirds of nannies are). If not, the nanny will probably expect you, the employer, to cover the costs of registration and associated requirements, as it's you who will benefit from the tax breaks and benefits! The exception to this is public liability insurance, which must be arranged and paid for by the nanny, as you wouldn't be able to claim against a policy you'd purchased yourself.

Ofsted inspects 10 per cent of childcarers on the voluntary register each year, although the inspector does not need to see the nanny with the children, and parents can refuse the inspector access to their home and/or family, which Ofsted must respect.

Find out more about voluntary registration for nannies in England at: **www.tinies.com** and **www.regulationmatters.co.uk**

Rules around voluntary registration in other parts of the UK vary. In Wales, nannies may register with the CSSIW's Voluntary Approval Scheme: **www.cssiw.org.uk** (search for 'nannies')

In Scotland, they can register with an agency that is itself registered with the Care Inspectorate (which makes it difficult to employ a nanny independently of an agency if you want to use childcare vouchers): **www.careinspectorate.com**

In Northern Ireland, they can register with the Home Childcarer Approval Scheme: **www.nidirect.gov.uk/home-childcarers**

Finding a nanny

You should begin searching for a nanny at least six weeks, and ideally up to three months, before you need them to start working for you, to give yourself time to find the right person, and for them to work their notice period in their current job. Start by making a list of your requirements. As well as deciding whether you want a daily or residential nanny, the days and hours you need and how much you will pay, other things to consider include:

- Is there a minimum level of training or childcare experience you'd expect your nanny to have?
- Are there any specialist skills or experience you'd like in your nanny? (For example dealing with a particular medical condition or dietary requirement?)
- Do you want your nanny to be able to drive?
- Do you mind if your nanny has a child of their own? (And would you allow them to care for their child alongside yours?)
- Does your nanny need to care for, or share your home with, any pets?
- Do you mind if your nanny smokes outside of working hours?
- Do you mind if your nanny's first language isn't the same as yours?
- Do you want a nanny who shares your religious or ethical beliefs?

As with all forms of paid childcare, word-of-mouth can be a good way of finding a nanny. Or, if you're happy to take on a newly qualified nanny, you could ask at your local college for details of recent graduates. The most common ways of finding a nanny, however, are through agencies and private ads.

Nanny agencies
A good nanny agency will take much of the hard work out of your nanny hunt, matching your family's needs with the CVs of nannies on its books, and carrying out essential background checks on your behalf. Nanny agencies vary enormously, so do a little research to find one that suits

your requirements. Before you sign up to an agency, find out:

- whether they cover a particular geographical area or childcare specialism – there are agencies providing bilingual nannies, nannies for newborns, male nannies, nannies for children with special needs, nannies who want to work overseas, and more!
- what sort of checks they carry out on their nannies (do they verify each nanny's ID, qualifications, right to work in the UK, driving licence and insurance, first aid training and enhanced Disclosure and Barring Service check, for example?)
- whether they will provide you and your nanny with ongoing support after a placement is made
- whether they offer any additional services, such as nanny payroll management or childcare training
- what fee they charge for a successful placement and when it's payable (some charge a flat rate, while others ask for a fee equivalent to 10 or 15 per cent of the nanny's annual salary, or four to six times their weekly pay. Check whether any salary-based fees are based on net or gross earnings, and whether you need to pay VAT on top.)
- what sort of guarantee or replacement policy they offer (many agencies will provide a replacement nanny for no extra fee if the first leaves after only a few weeks in the job).

The BAPN recommends that parents always double-check information provided by nanny agencies and follow up all references. A reputable agency will often be part of the Recruitment and Employment Confederation (**www.rec.uk.com**) or the Association of Nanny Agencies (**www.anauk.org**).

Private advertisements

If you don't mind doing a lot of the legwork yourself, you can avoid agency fees by finding a nanny through a private ad. Traditionally, nanny jobs were often advertised in The Lady magazine, local newspapers or cards in shop windows, but these days parents looking for nannies, and

nannies looking for work, are far more likely to use websites such as:
www.nannyjob.co.uk
www.childcare.co.uk
www.findababysitter.com
www.gumtree.co.uk.

Some of these websites charge a fee (normally around £20 to £25) for placing an ad. Others allow you to place and browse ads for free, but charge if you want to send a message to another site user.

Wherever you place your ad, include as much information as possible about the job to attract suitable candidates and put off those not right for the role. If you place a recruitment ad on any of the major nanny employment websites, you may be inundated with applications and sorting the good from the bad could be a huge task. Also, once you have a favourite candidate or candidates, you will need to carry out all the background checks that a nanny agency would (see above).

Interviewing a nanny

When interviewing for a nanny (especially for the first time), you may find it helpful to have someone else with you, to ensure you cover all the essentials and give a second opinion on the candidates. Let the interviewees know in advance what paperwork you would like to see – for example their CV, work visa, written references, referees' contact details, a photograph, photo-ID, diplomas and first aid certificates. It's usual for the interviewer to offer to cover the interviewees' expenses.

Allow around an hour for each interview, plus some time afterwards for discussion and notes. Ask all the interviewees the same questions and jot down their answers, as well as details such as what they were wearing and your first impressions, to help jog your memory later.

It's usually best to conduct the interviews in your own home, so that you can also show the nanny the parts of the house where she or he will be working (and living, if a residential nanny). If a face-to-face interview isn't possible, then use Skype rather than the phone to get a feel for your nanny's character and attitude, and to show them your home.

You probably won't want your children present throughout every interview, but letting them meet each candidate for a few minutes at the end will allow your little ones to give their opinion and let you see how they and the nanny respond to one another. Once you've whittled down your choice to one or two favourite candidates, invite them back for a second 'working interview' or paid trial day with your children present so that you can get a feel for how each nanny would perform in the role.

Questions you might want to ask at a first interview

About the nanny...

- How long have you been a nanny, and why did you choose nannying as a career?
- What do you like best about the job? And what do you like least?
- Tell me about your current (or most recent) position? Why are you leaving? (Or why did you leave?)
- What training and qualifications do you have? And how do you keep your skills and knowledge up to date?
- Do you belong to any professional associations or nanny groups?
- Are you registered with Ofsted (in England, or other registration schemes in other parts of the UK?) If not, would you be prepared to register?
- Describe your ideal family to work for.
- What are you most proud of in your career as a nanny?
- What do you find most challenging about working with children?
- What are your future career plans?

About your children...

- Do you have experience of caring for children the same age(s) as mine? (And with the same needs as mine?)
- What sort of activities would you do with my child(ren)? And what sort of toys and equipment do you like to have available?

- Where do you like to take children out and about?
- Can you give some examples of meals and snacks you like to prepare for children?
- What do you consider to be unacceptable behaviour, and how do you deal with this?
- What are your views on…? (Ask about anything that's particularly important to you, such as children watching television, manners, sugary snacks, getting plenty of fresh air and exercise)
- Would you be happy to keep to our current routine of… (naps, meals, toddler groups, swimming lessons, etc)
- Do you have experience of dealing with …? (Ask about issues that are relevant to your children, such as weaning, potty training, fussy eating or todler tantrums)
- How would you record my child's day?
- Have you ever been in an emergency situation involving a child in your care? What happened, and how did you cope?

Practical considerations…
- How soon would you be able to start?
- Where do you live, and how would you get to work? (for a live-out nanny)
- Would you be willing to do some light, child-related chores? (Preparing their meals? Doing their laundry? Keeping their bedrooms, play areas and bathrooms clean?)
- Are you willing to do evening and weekend babysitting?
- How do you like to communicate with the parents you work with?
- Would you be willing to come on holiday with our family? Or to take your annual leave at the same time as ours?
- Do you drive? If so, would you be prepared to drive my child(ren) in your/my car during the working day? And have you ever been in an accident with a child in your care?
- What are your salary expectations? (if these haven't already been defined)

- How many sick days have you had in the past year?
- Are you a smoker?
- Do you have any medical conditions, family responsibilities or anything else I should be aware of that might have an impact on your ability to carry out your duties as a nanny?

For a live-in nanny
- What are your preferred arrangements for meals?
- Would you ever want to have a partner, friend or family member to stay?
- What do you like to do in your free time?

And finally
- Are there any questions you'd like to ask about the role or our family?

To comply with equal opportunities legislation, steer clear of asking questions about the nanny's age, race, religion, disability, sexual orientation or relationship status, either explicitly or by implication, unless directly relevant to their ability to carry out the job.

After the interview, you should keep all notes and paperwork for six months (in case of an accusation of discrimination), then destroy those of all unsuccessful candidates.

Employing a nanny

As always when finding someone to care for your children, your choice will be as much about gut instinct as about qualifications and experience. If you find a nanny who meets all your criteria, and most importantly feels 'right', secure their services quickly before somebody else does!

Before agreeing anything in writing, though, take time to fully check the nanny's references. Even if you have found your nanny through an agency that carries out reference checks, it's well worth phoning previous employers for a chat. Find out what they liked about the nanny, any problems they had, and why they parted company. Ask them to confirm employment dates and other information the nanny has given you.

Negotiating a contract

Once satisfied with your nanny's references, your next step is to negotiate a contract. If you are employing your nanny through an agency, they will probably help you with this. If not, there are companies you can pay to draw up a contract for you. Or, if you prefer to do things yourself, there are sample contracts available online or you can buy cheaply from PACEY: **www.pacey.org.uk/shop**. The contract should explain all aspects of the job, and the responsibilities and rights that both you and the nanny have. It forms a legally binding agreement between employer and employee, and gives both of you protection if any problems arise.

Suggested clauses to include are:

Terms of employment
 – The names of the employer and the nanny.*
 – The names and dates of birth of the children to be cared for.
 – The nanny's working days and hours.*
 – The address(es) the nanny will work at.*
 – The date employment will start.*
 – Details of any trial period.*
 – Holiday and leave allowances and arrangements.*
 – Any perks and benefits, such as use of a car, a mobile phone or gym membership.
 – The notice period required if either you or the nanny want to change or end the arrangement.*

Responsibilities
 – Childcare duties expected of the nanny.*
 – Any domestic duties expected of the nanny.*
 – Responsibilities for confidentiality on both sides.

– Definition of, and penalties for, gross misconduct (harming or endangering a child, stealing from the family, or a serious breach of confidentiality are typical examples of sackable offences).

House rules
– Details of the accommodation and facilities provided for a live-in nanny.
– Rules regarding visitors to the home.
– Rules around using household appliances and resources, such as the washing machine, broadband and food.
– Rules around smoking and alcohol.

Practical arrangements
– How the parent and nanny will communicate (eg a daily handover, daily diary and regular reviews).
– Arrangements regarding meals and snacks for the nanny and the children.
– What happens if the nanny is unwell (including entitlement to sick pay).
– What happens if you or the children are unwell.
– An agreed approach to behaviour management, including acceptable punishments.
– Permission for the nanny to take the children on outings, photograph or film them, administer medicines, apply suncream, bathe them, and any other activities where child protection could potentially be an issue.
– Plans for emergencies (for example to seek help from a neighbour or grandparent).
– How the nanny should raise any grievances.*

Payment
– Details of the wages to be paid, how often and by what method, such as by bank transfer or via a payroll agency (if possible, negotiate a

gross salary to be paid monthly as this makes payroll arrangements more straightforward and ensures you won't be liable to pay more if the nanny's tax code changes).*
- What (if any) additional payments will be made for evening babysitting or weekend childcare.
- Rates of pay for unplanned overtime.
- How expenses will be paid.
- Date of salary review.
- Pension arrangements (if applicable).*

* By law these points must be included in the contract.

You and the nanny should both sign and date two copies of the contract, and each keep one in a safe place. If there are any changes to the nanny's responsibilities or working conditions, update the contract and make sure you both sign and date the new version. If you and another family are jointly employing a nanny-share, you may want to get legal advice to ensure the contract is fair for everyone involved.

Employment rights

As your employee, your nanny has various rights, including to:
- A written contract stating their duties, responsibilities and employment conditions.
- Regular payslips showing gross pay, tax paid, and any other dedications made.
- Paid holiday. Full-time employees are entitled to at least 28 days' holiday a year, which normally includes eight public holidays. Part-time employees get a pro rata holiday allowance. (Bear in mind that if you want your nanny to provide childcare for your family while you are away on holiday, this won't count as annual leave for them.)
- A pay rate at least equivalent to the minimum wage (£7.20 an hour for over-25s, £6.70 for those aged 21 to 24, and £5.30 an hour for 18- to 20-year-olds in 2016/17).
- Sick pay (£88.45 a week in 2016/17), if she or he is unwell and unable

to work for four or more days in a row.
- Maternity pay and leave, and time off for antenatal appointments.
- Redundancy pay, if they work for you for more than two years.
- A P60 tax certificate at the end of each year, and a P45 when they leave your employment.

For more information on your responsibilities as an employer, check out the Government's guidance on:
- Employing staff for the first time: **www.gov.uk/employing-staff**
- Employing a nanny or au pair:
  www.gov.uk/au-pairs-employment-law/nannies

Did you know?

As nannies are classed as 'domestic servants in private houses' they are normally exempt from the maximum 48-hour working week that most employees are entitled to. Even so, if you expect your nanny to work for longer than this, you should be very clear about the working hours upfront, and make absolutely sure your nanny is willing to work the hours you want.

Insurance

Before your nanny starts working for you, you must have employer's liability insurance cover of at least £5m. This will help pay compensation if the nanny is injured or becomes ill as a result of working for you. The good news is that employer's liability cover of £5m or even £10m for domestic staff is often included as standard as part of your home contents insurance. Check your policy, and ask your insurance provider if you are unsure.

It's important to let your home insurance provider know that you are taking on a nanny in any case. If you don't, and the insurance company later discovered that an employee was living in your house or had keys to the property, you could invalidate any claim on your insurance policy.

In addition, your nanny should have public liability insurance in case your child is injured or damages anyone else's property while in their care. They should arrange and pay for this themselves – ask to see their insurance certificate.

If your nanny will be driving as part of their job, it's also essential that they have suitable car insurance. If they will be driving a car that you own, try to add them to your own policy as a named business-use driver. Some insurers won't accept an additional driver who is very young, has a non-UK licence or has only recently passed their driving test, particularly if you have a high performance vehicle, so you may need to shop around. If your nanny will be using their own car to drive your children, make sure their car insurance covers them for business use, and offer to cover any additional costs involved.

Welcoming and settling in your nanny

It's usually helpful for your nanny to have a few days to settle in before she or he takes sole charge of your children. This gives you all a chance to get to know one another, and lets your nanny get used to your home, your family's routine and the way you like to do things.

There are lots of things your nanny will want to learn in those first few days...

- **About your children** – What are their favourite toys, books, activities, songs and TV programmes? Do they have any comfort items or habits? What foods do they like and dislike? Do they have any nicknames or unusual words for things? Are there any medicines or other treatments they need regularly? Are they allergic to anything?
- **About your day** – What times do you leave for work and come home again? What times do the children get up, have meals and snacks, go to preschool or school, have naps, attend activities or classes, have baths and go to bed? Are there any regular visitors to the house,

such as granny, or a cleaner or gardener?

- **About your home** – Have you shown the nanny how to operate appliances such as your washing machine, tumble drier, oven, microwave and satellite TV? How about your locks, alarms and heating systems? Where are food, dishes, cleaning products, toys, nappies, children's clothes and spare bedding kept? Are there any pets, and does the nanny need to take any responsibility for them? How should the nanny deal with phone calls and personal callers to the house? Are there any parts of the home that are out of bounds? Have you discussed the house rules?
- **About the equipment you use** – Does the nanny know how to use your steriliser, stairgates and baby monitor? Can they open and collapse the buggy, and use any car seats safely? Do they feel confident driving your car, if this will be part of their job?
- **About the local area** – Where are the best places to take children and/ or meet other nannies? Where do the children attend school, preschool or classes? Where's the nearest supermarket or convenience store? Are there any parking restrictions or speed traps to be aware of?
- **Dealing with emergencies** – Where are the stop cock, fuse board and torches, in case of a problem with the water or electricity? Are there neighbours, friends or family members that the nanny can call on in an emergency? Does the nanny have mobile and work numbers for you and your partner, and contact details of professionals such as the doctor, dentist and vet?

Putting the key points in writing will help avoid any misunderstandings. Be firm about the issues that matter to you most, and try to stay relaxed about those that aren't so critical.

No childcarer will do things in exactly the same way as you, and that's fine. What's important is that your children are safe, content and well cared for.

Most nannies fill in a daily diary or record sheet for the parents they work for, giving information about what children have had to eat and drink, nappy changes or toileting, sleep, activities and any observations. Many are also happy to take photos or snippets of film at parents' request. Before they start work, discuss with your nanny the best way(s) of recording your child's day and sharing information.

A good nanny should carry out a risk assessment on their workplace before taking sole charge of children there, so don't be offended if they point out something that needs repairing or ask for a safety device to be installed. You could help them by asking if they think there's anything that could be improved from a safety point of view.

The handover should become part of your daily routine once the nanny takes full charge of the children. Allowing ten or fifteen minutes at the beginning and end of each day for a catch-up will help you both maintain a positive working relationship and address any minor concerns before they become problems.

You should carry out a fuller review, if possible without the children present, at the end of the nanny's trial or probationary period, and every three to six months afterwards.

For more information about employing a nanny:

British Association of Professional Nannies
www.bapn.org.uk 01622 815271

Norland Nannies
www.norland.co.uk

Professional Association for Childcare and Early Years:
www.pacey.org.uk 0303 003 0005

'I never imagined that I would ever employ a nanny (what an extravagance!) but as I have twins it worked out cheaper and easier than any other arrangement. Our nanny took over before I left in the morning. I didn't have to get the children fed, washed and dressed and transported to another venue and I didn't have to pick them up, so the arrangement was really convenient. We chose our nanny because our children were drawn to her immediately. She was fun and full of energy, spoke to the boys at their level and she clearly loved children. She spoke clear English, which was important to us as the boys were just learning to talk. She also had experience of having sole charge for twin babies, and was a super cook too. She took the boys to lots of local activities, arranged play dates, and they loved travelling on the bus with her. Go with your instinct – you will know whether the nanny is the right person for you or not. If you don't find anyone immediately, keep trying until you find someone you are happy with. Let your children meet the candidates at the interview too – you'll see clearly whether the nanny is natural with them.'
– *Sandra, trade union legal officer and mother of two*

'Our elder son went to nursery. When our daughter was born we switched to a nanny, mainly because it fit better with our work patterns – we needed a lot of flexibility. I also liked having the kids looked after at home. Logistics are so much easier. I didn't have to worry if one of them was ill because they could simply stay at home if need be, which was a huge weight off my mind. Our first nanny wanted to study to qualify as a teacher, and nannying allowed her to do that. We choose her mainly because we thought she would fit in well with our family, and she was obviously a "self-starter" who was comfortable taking the initiative. The right nanny is worth her weight in gold, and I mean that literally because nannies are an expensive childcare option! That said, once you have two or three children a nanny compares favourably with nursery fees. Be prepared to work at the employer/employee relationship. It is sometimes hard to find the time when you are also juggling work and home, but it really does pay off.'

– *Eleanor, lawyer and mother of three*

I found my nanny by posting an ad on the website www.childcare. co.uk. I chose her because she took such an immediate and genuine interest in my son, and because her values are close to mine. She's gone into nannying as a second career after raising three children, and her experience and maturity instil confidence in me. She extended her duties semi-voluntarily over the years. At first she would prepare my son's meals and do some ironing while he napped. Off her own bat she began doing things like taking him to the library, changing the bed linen and putting the bins out, and now she prepares our evening meal while he's at preschool on a Wednesday, which is lovely! Because she also works for other families, she's self-employed and so I don't have to deal with her tax and National Insurance. My son loves her and I couldn't do my job without her. I always tell people she's like my wife!'

– *Lara, management consultant and mother of one*

I wanted a nanny as my son was only a year old when I returned to work, and I wanted him to be cared for in a home environment for his first years. I also wanted to make sure he would have a good sleep during the day, home-cooked vegetarian meals and trips out. Our nanny-share arrangement means he has someone to socialise with and is learning how to share. The nanny takes the children to regular playgroups and on play dates, and teaches them new things. It's also cheaper – a normal nanny in our area charges £10 per hour net; the

nanny-share is £6 each. We found our nanny through an agency. She had good references, had worked with multiple children before, and was friendly and nice. I'm really happy with our choice. Childcare isn't stressful at all as she's so reliable and flexible. There's no hassle of dropping our son off or picking him up – she just continues wherever you are in the morning. So if you haven't finished dressing the baby, she will. And if you need a babysitter she'll do that too. Both families are registered as employers, with two separate contracts. She works one week at our house and then the next at my friend's, who only lives two streets away. We have a travel cot in a separate bedroom for my friend's baby, an extra high-chair, and we bought a double buggy between us. Whoever is 'on' that week pays for food and nappies, and we use a nanny tax firm to sort out payslips and taxes.'
– *Yvonne, business analyst and mother of one*

Chapter 5

Au pairs

Support with childcare and light household duties as part of a cultural exchange

An au pair is a young person from overseas who helps out with childcare and light housework while living in your home as part of your family. An au pair can't be expected to have sole responsibility for a baby or toddler, but may be a good childcare option if your children are older or you simply need a little help at home.

An au pair lives with your family and does some childcare and light household duties in return for weekly pocket money. The arrangement allows the au pair to study English and learn about British culture, while you and your family benefit from having extra help around the house.

The au pair cultural exchange programme began in Europe after the Second World War, when the changing economic times meant fewer families could afford domestic staff and more young women needed to earn a living. The term 'au pair' is French for 'on a par' or 'equal to', the idea being that the au pair lives as an equal member of your family.

Au pairs are young people, aged 18-plus, who are unmarried and have no dependants. Most have no childcare training, and many have never looked after children or had sole charge of a household before. The proportion of men is a little higher than in other forms of childcare – around 13 per cent of au pairs are male, according to a Recruitment and Employment Confederation study.

Rather than earning a wage, au pairs have their board and lodgings and a 'pocket money' allowance (currently around £70 to £90 a week) provided by the family they live with. This means that, unlike nannies, they are not generally classed as employees, and the parents they work for are not their employers. Current UK Government guidance states that, for a young person to be classed as an au pair, most of the following must apply:

- they're a foreign national living with a family in the UK
- they're an EU citizen or have entered the UK on a Youth Mobility Visa or student visa
- they're here on a cultural exchange programme
- they've got a signed letter of invitation from the host family that includes details of their stay, eg accommodation, living conditions, approximate working hours, free time, pocket money
- they learn about British culture from the host family and share their own culture with them
- they have their own private room in the house, provided free of charge
- they eat their main meals with the host family, free of charge
- they help with light housework and childcare for around 30 hours a week, including a couple of evenings babysitting
- they get reasonable pocket money
- they can attend English language classes at a local college in their spare time
- they're allowed time to study and can practise their English with the host family
- they sometimes go on holiday with the host family and help look after the children
- they can travel home to see their family during the year.

Source: www.gov.uk/au-pairs-employment-law/au-pairs

A young person from a country in the European Economic Area (EEA) or European Free Trade Association (EFTA) does not need a visa or work permit to become an au pair in the UK. (Although au pairs from Croatia are still subject to some restrictions as they have only recently joined the EEA.) People aged 18 to 30 from Australia, Canada, New Zealand, Japan, Hong Kong, the Republic of Korea, Taiwan and Monaco may become au pairs under the Tier 5 Youth Mobility Scheme. They will need a visa and must meet certain other requirements, including registering at a police station within seven days of arriving in the UK.

A young person who comes from a country outside of the EEA and EFTA and is not covered by the Tier 5 scheme may be able to work as an au pair on a student visa. In this case, they must meet certain criteria, including proving that they are enrolled on an English course and can afford their stay in the UK.

Some au pairs work as an 'au pair plus', meaning they are on duty for 35 hours a week and receive a weekly allowance of around £90–£110. If your au pair earns more than the Lower Earnings Limit, £112 a week in 2016/17, you must register with HMRC as their employer.

Remember that the au pair's allowance isn't the only cost involved. Once you've factored in the extra grocery shopping, cooking, laundry, energy costs, travel or petrol and phone use involved, as well as one-off costs such as preparing the au pair's room, insurances and agency or search fees, you will probably be spending at least double what you pay the au pair in pocket money.

Au pairs are not trained childcare professionals, and many have no previous experience of looking after children at all. They may also have never lived away from home before, and their knowledge of household management and of the English language, British way of life and local area may be very limited.

For these reasons, **au pairs are not permitted to have sole charge of children under the age of two, and the Family and Childcare Trust recommends that they do not have sole charge of children aged under four**. For your own peace of mind, you will probably not want to leave your child with an au pair until they are old enough to tell you about their day, communicate clearly with the au pair and seek help if needed.

An au pair should never be considered a cheap substitute for a nanny, but may be a great childcare choice if you need after-school or holiday care for older children, or if you are a stay-at-home parent or work from home and want somebody to supervise and play with your children when you are busy.

Some families have unrealistic, even exploitative, expectations of an au pair's working hours and duties. In 2014 a Birkbeck study of ads placed by parents on www.gumtree.com found them wanting an au pair to work for an average of just under 39 hours a week, for average weekly pay of £108.

What are the advantages of using an au pair?

- The care is often more affordable and flexible than that provided by a trained childcarer.
- An au pair should help family life to run more smoothly, not least for all those times when you wish you could be doing two things at once.
- The care is provided in your own home, so the children have access to their toys and other belongings, and siblings of different ages can be cared for together.
- An au pair may be a good short-term childcare option, for example if you just need care while your children are on their summer holiday from school or preschool.
- Your children may learn some of the au pair's native language.
- Children often enjoy having a carer who seems more like an older cousin than an authority figure, and you may be able to find an au pair who shares their interest in sport, music or other hobbies.
- You and your family may enjoy sharing your home with a young adult from a different country, learning about their culture and language, and teaching them about yours.
- Recent economic difficulties in some European countries have led to more qualified and experienced young people seeking work as au pairs in the UK.

And what are the disadvantages?

- Au pairs usually have no formal childcare training and are not parents themselves, so are unlikely to know much about matters such as child development, infant nutrition and child protection.
- Having a stranger living in your house can feel intrusive and may put a strain on the family.

- Your au pair may not be able to speak, read or write English very well which, as well as causing misunderstandings, could be confusing for your children and not good for little ones' language development.
- You won't be able to use childcare vouchers or the new tax-free childcare scheme, or claim the childcare element of Working Tax Credit or Universal Credit, unless your au pair is prepared to register with Ofsted in England (or other bodies in other parts of the UK) and meets all the requirements regarding training and insurance (see page 153).
- It can be difficult to check references and verify other documents if these are in a foreign language, unless you go through an au pair agency who will do this for you.
- You probably won't get a chance to meet your au pair in person before they come and live with you.
- You may discover cultural differences around mealtimes, routine, discipline, personal hygiene and more.
- Many au pairs have no experience of household management, so you need to be prepared to show them exactly how to do every chore and work every appliance.
- An au pair who's never lived away from home before may be very homesick or might exploit their new-found freedoms. Either way, their behaviour could be stressful and time-consuming, and you may feel that you are responsible for an additional child.
- You may be irritated or concerned about what your au pair does in their free time – too much partying, sleeping or taking on another job, for example.
- A young or inexperienced au pair may find it hard to maintain authority over your children.
- If you want a childcarer who can drive your children, bear in mind that a young au pair may not be an experienced driver, may not have driven a right-hand drive car or on the left-hand side of the road before, and may be extremely expensive to insure. (See page 107 for more on au pairs driving.)

- As most au pairs stay with a family for just six to twelve months, you may feel that you are in a perpetual recruitment cycle, and your children may not like having a succession of different carers.

How can I find a good au pair?

As with nannies, a few families are lucky enough to find a good au pair through word-of-mouth, but most use an agency or an online matching service.

Au pair agencies

Just like a nanny agency, an au pair agency will take a lot of the hard work out of finding the right candidate for your job – at a price. Some charge a registration fee, others just for a successful placement. Either way, expect to pay around £300 to £500, depending on your requirements and how long the au pair will be with you.

Before you sign up, make sure you're clear about the services the agency will provide. They should give you a selection of candidates to choose from, all matched to your family's requirements. Ideally, you will get an introductory letter from each prospective au pair (and possibly a video too), as well as a photo, references (usually one character reference and one outlining their suitability to work with children), confirmation from a medical professional that they are fit to work with young children, and confirmation of a criminal record check. The agency should also help with any bureaucracy, and offer support for au pairs and parents if the arrangement runs into any difficulties.

Some agencies meet all their au pairs in person before placing them, or work closely with counterpart agencies in other countries who carry out vetting procedures. Some offer au pairs training in first aid and basic childcare, or organise excursions and social events for their au pairs. And some will provide a replacement au pair for no extra fee if things don't work out with the first for any reason.

Even if you use an agency, it's advisable to interview your au pair over Skype and check their references before taking them on.

A good agency will probably be a member of the British Au Pair

Agencies Association (BAPAA – **www.bapaa.org.uk**) or the Recruitment and Employment Confederation (REC– **www.rec.uk.com**).

Online matching services

Using an online matching service gives you a vast array of au pairs to choose from, and for a far lower fee, but is more time-consuming and more of a lottery. Many au pair sites will allow you to browse posts for free, but you may pay to place your own ad or to send messages to other site users.

Probably the best known international au pair matching site is the German **www.aupairworld.com**, which charges around €40 for a month's membership. **www.gumtree.com** is also a popular hunting ground for au pairs.

Placing an ad on any of the major au pair websites could leave you inundated with hundreds of responses. Make your advert as detailed as possible and be very specific about your requirements – regarding age, nationality, skills, experience and interests, for example – to help to limit the number of applicants.

If you are thinking of taking on an au pair through a matching website, carefully check their medical certificate, police check and references. An interview via Skype is also helpful, as it allows you to get a good idea of the au pair's personality and proficiency in English, and to show them your home, their accommodation and introduce them to your children. Take a look at this section in the book on interviewing nannies (page 84) for ideas of questions to ask.

Beware of scams targeting parents who use online au pair matching services. In particular, be wary of any prospective childcarer who asks for money upfront for any reason. Another risk of finding an au pair online is having your selected candidate pull out at the last minute because they've been offered more money or better working conditions by another family. It's little wonder that some parents say the process is more nerve-wracking than internet dating!

Drawing up a contract

An au pair's contract is often described as an 'invitation letter', and if they are from outside Europe they will need to have it before arriving in the UK. The contract or invitation letter details the au pair's duties, weekly allowance, accommodation, arrangements for meals, start date, duration of placement (if known), working hours, time off, notice period (usually two weeks), benefits and any holiday entitlement. You can find model au pair contracts online, or take a look at the section of this book on nanny contracts (page 88) for more ideas of things to include (bearing in mind that the hours, duties and expectations will be slightly different for an au pair).

Current Government guidance states: 'Au pairs usually live with the family they work for and are unlikely to be classed as a worker or an employee. They aren't entitled to the National Minimum Wage or paid holidays.' However, since 2010 the BAPAA has recommended that au pairs should have the minimum holiday entitlement that other UK workers enjoy – 28 days a year, including eight public holidays.

The employment status of au pairs can be something of a grey area. If their earnings cross the lower earnings limit, which is £112 a week in 2016/17, you technically become the au pair's employer, and must register with HMRC, submit payroll reports and comply with employment laws. Complications may also arise if your au pair takes on work outside the home, either during their time with you or afterwards. The pocket money you pay could be classed as earnings, in which case you will want to be the au pair's primary employer for tax and NI purposes so that you get the benefit of the au pair's tax-free allowance. If you have any questions or concerns, speak to a legal or tax advisor.

Preparing for your au pair's arrival

Your au pair should have their own private room in your home, in a good decorative state with a bed, wardrobe, table or desk and natural light. As well as the au pair's food and drink, you should supply basic toiletries such as shampoo, soap and tissues. Many families also provide their au pair with a TV, stereo and access to broadband, and some offer perks such as a private bathroom, mobile phone, travelcard or gym membership.

Before your au pair arrives, let your home insurance company know that there will be an additional adult living in your house, and amend your vehicle insurance if the au pair will be driving your car. If your au pair is from the EEA they will be able to use NHS services free of charge, as long as they have their European Health Insurance Card (EHIC). Au pairs from other countries will need to arrange suitable medical insurance, and all au pairs are advised to have travel insurance.

Your au pair should arrange and pay for their own travel to the UK, but it's usual for the host family to meet them at the airport, station or port. Involve your children as much as possible in preparations for their new au pair's arrival. They may want to make a welcome card or plan a special meal or outing for their new carer.

Welcoming your au pair

It's important to allow plenty of time to help your au pair settle in to their new role. They may know very little about caring for children or housework, and probably nothing about the local area, so you'll have lots to show them.

Take them through all the points outlined in the nanny induction section of this book (see page 92), remembering that everyday tasks such as changing a nappy, preparing children's tea or even using a washing machine, dishwasher or vacuum cleaner may be new to your au pair. As well as showing them the local area, you'll also want to help them register with a GP and perhaps a dentist too, open a bank account, and register with the local police station if they're from outside Europe. If you know other au pairs or young people of a similar age, introduce them so that your au pair can start to make friends.

If your au pair will be driving as part of their role, familiarise them with your car and make sure they are confident driving on the left. The BAPAA recommends that host families arrange driving lessons for their au pair and spend time in the car with them to get them used to British cars and British roads. Au pairs from the EEA can drive in the UK without restriction. Those from other countries can use their national driving licence for up to twelve months, and may find it helpful to get an international driving permit that can be easily understood by authorities.

Some parents like to prepare a handbook or folder for the au pair, full of useful information such as the family's daily and weekly timetable, emergency contact details, instructions for appliances, maps of the local area, information about places to visit, and so on. You should also give a written set of house rules, covering issues such as meals and snacks, drinking and smoking, privacy and confidentiality, house guests, and use of the TV, broadband, phone and stereo. Most experienced au pair hosts agree that it's best to start strict and relax the rules a little later if appropriate – it's much harder to get tough later on.

Further information

British Au Pair Agencies Association
www.bapaa.org.uk 07946 149916

Au Pair World
www.aupairworld.com

Full details of the European au pair scheme are set out in the Council of Europe's European Agreement on Au Pair Placement:
www.coe.int/en/web/conventions/full-list/-/conventions/treaty/068

Student childcarers

Some families seek out local college or university students to provide childcare – most commonly for school-aged children during school holidays. Like au pairs, student childcarers are generally unregistered and unexperienced, so if you're considering this kind of care, much of the information in this chapter will be relevant.

'We've had four au pairs so far. I love the flexibility, for example getting more help around the house than we did with a nanny, and last-minute babysitting too. It is much more of a lottery than hiring a nanny though. With a nanny you can interview and interview until you find one that's just right. With an au pair it's often a Skype conversation with someone whose English isn't great. I've found our au pairs through an agency specialising in French-speaking au pairs, as well as through AuPairWorld and Gumtree. I always choose au pairs who are aged at least 22 and have already lived away from home. And I never leave them alone with my children until I've spent at least two weeks getting to know them and making sure I feel comfortable with them. The current arrangement is a great success. The children clearly love our au pair and missed her enormously when we recently went on holiday without her.'

– *Hannah, accountant and mother of two*

'We find that having an au pair brings far more benefits for our money than any other form of support. We are lucky enough to have the space to accommodate one, with a spare bedroom and bathroom. I think many more families would consider this kind of opportunity if they had more space. The flexibility is a real bonus with a young family. Most au pairs sign up to be available for two evenings' babysitting each week and that gives my wife and I back a little of the spontaneity we lost on becoming parents. I can come in from a long day and ask her if she wants to go out and, in the main, having a fantastic, understanding au pair means we can.'

– *Al, company director and father of three*

'When my girls were very young I always used an agency to find my nannies and our first au pair. Now I use the website AuPairWorld or word of mouth. I prefer to have eastern European au pairs who are aged 24+ as I find they look at it more as a job rather than just a holiday. The best things about having an au pair are the flexibility it offers, the fact someone is in the house every day to tidy up, and the affordability too. The downside is having someone hanging around in the evenings when you just want to spend time with your husband! I always interview on Skype but it's far from easy and I've made my fair share of mistakes. I will now only have au pairs who speak very good English, as its tough on the children when they can't communicate properly with the person looking after them. My girls love having an au pair and are always very welcoming, wanting to show them stuff and do things with them. Communication is crucial. Give instructions to the minutest detail and have lots of patience. Once they get it, they are fantastic. Those that haven't "got it" by three months have tended to leave.'

– *Megan, investment manager and mother of three*

'I have experience of working with young people, which I think makes me realistic in my expectations of an au pair, and realistic too about the support and time I need to put in to make the relationship blossom for us all. The au pair programme is a cultural exchange and not simply cheap labour. Anyone who views it as the latter is far more likely to have a poor experience. The shared learning about other cultures, customs and beliefs benefits all of us. Any young person, living and working in another tongue, in another country will need support. If you can treat an au pair as you would want another family to treat your own child working similarly abroad you'll be going a long way to developing a relationship that will reap rewards for you both.'

– *Gemma, property developer and mother of three*

Chapter 6

Family childcare

Convenient childcare provided by someone you and your child love and trust

Parents often see family care – usually provided by their or their partner's parents – as the perfect solution to their childcare needs. After all, the family member already knows and loves your child and has a genuine interest in making sure they receive the best possible care. And, whether it takes place in your home or theirs, the care will be in a setting where your child already feels comfortable and at ease. Family childcare is often the cheapest option too, as many family members charge little or nothing for their childcare services, and no other form of childcare is likely to be as flexible if you work shifts or your child is poorly. But using family childcare can also present some unique challenges.

According to 2013 research by Age UK and Grandparents Plus, one in four families depends on a grandparent to meet all or some of their childcare needs while working, and 63 per cent of grandparents look after their grandchildren some of the time, whether providing full daycare, nursery pick-ups, sickness cover, school holiday care, evening babysitting, or just a little respite at weekends. Even grandparents who live a long way from their grandchildren may provide care, perhaps staying with the family for a night or two each week or during school holidays.

The two charities have calculated that grandparent childcare saves UK families £7.3bn a year in formal care costs. Countless more hours of care are provided by other family members, such as aunts and uncles, step-grandparents and great-grandparents.

When it's possible logistically and all parties are willing, family care can be an excellent childcare option, with children receiving plenty of one-to-one attention from a carer who's genuinely interested in their development and wellbeing. But some family members may feel put-upon and resentful at having to provide care, while others may not be physically capable of fully meeting a young child's needs.

Being left to their own devices, or sitting in front of the TV or in the buggy or car for hours on end, is a poor substitute for all the stimulation and learning opportunities a professional childcarer would provide. If you're considering asking a family member to provide childcare, think carefully about whether it would be in their best interests and those of your child.

What are the advantages of family childcare?

- **Reassurance** – your childcare provider is someone close to you or your partner, and who is probably already involved in your child's life.
- **Convenience** – whether the childcare takes place in your home or that of your family member, it will be an environment that's familiar to your child and where they can have access to their toys and belongings.
- **Affordability** – Grandparents Plus says the majority of grandparents don't charge for the care they provide. Of those who do accept payment, many charge much less than the going rate for formal childcare. And of course there are no deposits, retainer fees or lateness penalties to worry about.
- **Flexibility** – a family member is more likely to be able to care for a child who's feeling a bit under the weather, provide care in the evenings or at weekends, or cover a last-minute change to your work arrangements, than a nursery or childminder.
- **Family bonds** – children regularly cared for by a family member often develop a particularly strong relationship with that person. The arrangement may also help your child develop a deeper understanding of their family history and cultural heritage, and provide security and reassurance when there's any sort of upheaval at home.

And what are the disadvantages?

- You're dependent on one person (or possibly two if it's a couple providing the care), so will need back-up if they're ill or on holiday.
- The childcarer is untrained and their working premises not formally inspected.
- Older family members may lack the energy and physical strength needed to care for a young child – or two, or three!
- Children may miss out on opportunities to mix with their peers or enjoy physical exercise.
- Your children's days will probably be less carefully planned and structured than with a professional childcarer.
- You may find the care is less reliable than with a professional child-carer, especially if you're paying little or nothing for it.
- Conflicts and resentment can arise over a range of issues, from money to diet to discipline.
- The family member may feel over-burdened or trapped by the arrangement.

Avoiding the possible pitfalls of family childcare...

Setting the ground rules

For any family childcare arrangement to be a success, it's essential to discuss ground rules in advance and review them regularly. Older family members' views on childcare may be outdated, or simply different to your own, so be upfront about your expectations. Emphasise the things that really matter to you, and be prepared to be more relaxed about those that aren't quite as important.

Among the issues to discuss before the childcare arrangement begins are:

- routine, including mealtimes, snack times, nap times and any classes or preschool sessions
- meals, snacks and drinks (do you have strong views about any aspect of your child's diet?)

- activities (what are your opinions on children watching TV or DVDs, or using computers, or having fresh air and exercise?)
- arrangements for pick-ups and drop-offs
- arrangements for payment and expenses
- arrangements for holidays and sickness – yours, your family member's and your child's
- discipline
- children's safety (see the section on 'Children's wellbeing' below).

It's also important to give your family member any phone numbers they may need, such as mobile and office numbers for you and your partner, and contact details for any preschool or formal childcare provider, and for your child's doctor, dentist and health visitor. Offer to put these into their phone, or make a list for the wall.

The Grandparents' Association has produced a Family Childcare Checklist to help families sort out the practicalities of an informal childcare arrangement: **www.grandparents-association.org.uk/childcare/childcare.html**

Before committing to any family childcare arrangement have a trial so that you can see how it suits you, your family member and your child, and agree any changes that might be necessary.

Review the arrangement regularly, ideally when your child isn't present so that you can have a full and frank discussion. If your child is approaching a milestone, such as weaning, toilet training or starting preschool, discuss in advance how you're both going to manage this.

If you want the family member to follow your rules, it's only reasonable to follow theirs too. This means being punctual with pick-ups and drop-offs, providing any food or equipment you've agreed to supply, and giving as much notice as possible of changes to the usual pattern of care.

Money matters

Don't assume the care provided by a family member will be free. Although the majority of family childcarers don't charge, others want or need payment, particularly if they've had to stop or cut down on other work to look after your child.

If you do pay your family member a regular fee for childcare, then they technically become your employee. This entitles them to certain rights and may make them liable for tax and National Insurance contributions, depending on how much you pay them and whether they have any other income. It also gives you responsibilities as their employer, in much the same way as if you were paying a nanny (see page 90)

As family childcarers are not registered, if your family member does charge you for their services you won't be able to claim the childcare element of Working Tax Credit or Universal Credit. Nor will you be able to claim childcare vouchers from your employer or take advantage of the tax-free childcare scheme (see page 159). The only exception to this is if your family member works as a registered childminder, also available to care for children from other families.

The financial aspects of having a grandparent care for your baby may change considerably, as the Government is considering extending the Shared Parental Leave scheme (see page 29) to grandparents from 2018.

One financial benefit already available to grandparents and others who have stopped working to care for a family member aged under 12 is Specified Adult Childcare Credits, commonly known as 'Grandparent Credits'. These are National Insurance contribution credits that help family childcarers who are below retirement age to build up entitlement to state pension and some bereavement benefits. Your family member won't get them automatically – they'll need to claim by filling in a form CA9176. Find out more by calling the National Insurance helpline on 0300 200 3500 or visiting: **www.gov.uk** (search for 'CA9176').

Family childcare could save you thousands, or even tens of thousands, of pounds over the years. If your family member refuses payment you'll want to find some way of thanking them, perhaps by buying them gifts, arranging treats, or offering some practical help such as gardening or decorating in return.

You'll also want to make sure that caring for your child doesn't leave your family member out-of-pocket. Discuss in advance how you're going to cover the many costs involved, including:

- meals, snacks, drinks and baby milk
- nappies, wipes, sun cream and toiletries
- petrol or transport fares
- costs for activities and outings
- toys, books and safety equipment.

You could supply all of these up-front, ask your family member to keep a monthly tally of expenses, or provide a kitty of money that they dip into whenever they need to pay for anything child-related.

If your family member will be caring for your child in their own home, they'll need appropriate equipment – a highchair, cot or travel-cot, buggy, car seat, stair gate and changing mat, for example – which you should offer to provide.

Websites such as eBay and Gumtree, NCT sales and Facebook selling groups are great for cheap pre-used equipment, but bear in mind that safety organisations advise against using second-hand cot mattresses and car seats.

Did you know?

The official definition of family childcare is very broad. According to the government's guidance on Specified Adult Childcare Credits (see opposite), as well as grandparents it includes great-grandparents and great-great-grandparents, aunts and uncles, brothers and sisters (whether full siblings, step siblings, half siblings or adopted siblings), as well as the spouses, partners, civil partners, former partners or children of any of these people.

Children's wellbeing

Young children whose grandparents provide childcare, especially in wealthier families, tend to have better vocabularies and be more emotionally secure than their peers in any other sort of childcare, according to a 2009 study by the Institute of Education. On the downside, however, children cared for by grandparents tend to mix less with their peers, have less developed social skills, and don't perform quite as well in tests of school-readiness (recognising numbers, letters, colours and shapes for example), compared to those who attend centre-based care.

Make sure your child doesn't miss out on early learning by providing your family childcarer with some educational toys, books and activity ideas. You can also help your child develop the social skills they'll need for preschool and school by encouraging your family member to take them to playgrounds and toddler groups (in some areas there are groups specifically for grandparents caring for grandchildren). You might also want to involve your child in group activities on days when you're not working.

A UK study in 2010, reported in the International Journal of Obesity, found that children cared for by their grandparents part time were 15 per cent more likely to be overweight, and those in full-time grandparent childcare were 34 per cent more likely to be overweight, than their peers in paid-for childcare. This is probably because grandparents are more likely to indulge children with unhealthy treats and less likely to ensure they have plenty of exercise than professional childcarers. The study found the problem particularly affected more affluent and educated families.

If you think too much unhealthy food or too little physical activity could be an issue with your family childcare provider, have a chat with them before it becomes a problem. Agree some ground rules covering what sort of meals, drinks and snacks should be provided and how often. Talk about the physical activities your child enjoys too, and maybe arrange some opportunities for exercise, for example by paying for a trip to the softplay centre or swimming pool, providing outdoor toys such as footballs and scooters, or suggesting your child helps out with activities like gardening and dog-walking.

Safety is another issue to be aware of, especially if your family member will be caring for your child in their home. Help them to install child-proofing equipment, such as stair gates and cupboard locks. Make sure, too, that your child won't have unsupervised contact with unfamiliar adults visiting the home, such as your family member's friends or a handyman or gardener.

You may find it useful to do an informal risk assessment together, looking out for the sorts of hazards a childcare inspector might look for – are fires guarded, smoke alarms fitted, pet bowls and litter trays out of children's reach, ponds filled or covered, chemicals and tools locked away, and so on? US research suggests that poisoning by medicines may be a particular hazard for children cared for by grandparents, as older people are more likely to be on medication and less likely to store it in child-proof containers.

Organisations such as the Red Cross and St John Ambulance, and some Sure Start centres, run short first aid courses especially for people who care for young children, giving information on how to deal with choking, burns, falls and other situations that young children commonly get themselves into. For your peace of mind, you might want to arrange for your family member to attend one of these.

Grandparents' wellbeing

No matter how young-at-heart they are, your parents (or in-laws or grandparents) are unlikely to have the same energy and vitality they had when you were growing up 20, 30 or even 40 years ago. And no matter how willing they are, they may find caring for a fractious baby or keeping up with a lively toddler exhausting. In a 2013 survey, carried out by insurance group RIAS, 30 per cent of grandparent carers admitted finding the role tiring, and one in 12 wished they could do it less.

Before embarking on any regular childcare arrangement, you and your family member will want to be sure that they are physically up to the job. Can they lift your child and restrain them if necessary, carry the car seat, do up the buckles on the buggy and highchair, bathe your child if providing overnight care, and so on? Do some trial runs and agree to be open and honest with one another if either of you has any concerns about the physical side of things – either now, or in the future when your child is bigger and stronger, your family member may have more health concerns, and there may be more children to be cared for!

Your family member's mental health is just as important as their physical wellbeing. The Grandparents' Association has expressed concern about some grandparents feeling put-upon, taken for granted and stressed by their childcare responsibilities. Others may be resentful at the impact the arrangement has on their career, finances, social life or relationship with their partner.

On the plus side, there's evidence that providing part-time childcare may have health benefits for the older generation. A 2014 study by Grandparents Plus and King's College London found that grandparents who cared for their grandchildren for up to 15 hours a week tended to be in better health than their counterparts who provided no childcare, even when socio-economic background and existing health conditions were taken into account.

Family politics

Grandparent childcare may work perfectly for a first grandchild, but become increasingly problematic the more grandchildren that come along. Grandparents may feel pressured into offering their other children and grandchildren the same arrangement as for the first, leaving themselves over-stretched and over-burdened. Or they may not be able to provide the same level of childcare for all their children, for reasons of geography, health or simple practicality, creating feelings of guilt and causing jealousy and resentment among adult siblings.

Another area of possible conflict is between grandparents on different sides of the family. (Separations and remarriages mean children these days often have three or four sets.) Some parents find they have grandparents competing to provide childcare, and possibly over-indulging children with treats and toys in an effort to seem the 'best'.

In other families resentment can build because the grandparent providing childcare sees those who aren't as having fewer responsibilities and more free time. Or a grandparent who isn't able to offer childcare may be envious of one who is because of all the time and close relationship that the childcarer can enjoy with their grandchild.

It's also important to maintain your own relationship with your family member. Try to spend time with them apart from the children sometimes so that your contact is not solely about the children's care.

Whatever the situation in your family, it's important to be sensitive to everyone's feelings and needs, and to tackle any issues before rifts develop.

What parents say...

Our children have been able to build a lovely relationship with their grandparents as they see them every week. The kids like having their own toys and belongings, and being taken to parks, farms, softplay, etc. My parents and in-laws are willing to look after them if they are ill, and will swap with each other if they are ill. They also provide childcare at short notice and if we need to work late. We're very lucky.'
– James, costs lawyer and father of two

You need to have early discussions about requirements and expectations on both sides. Before you go back to work, let your children spend time with their grandparents while you are there, to build familiarity and so they can see how you look after them. I organised

for my mother and mother-in-law to do first aid training. I also made sure that on my days off I took my son to groups and playdates, and enrolled him in preschool as soon as he was old enough, so that he was able to spend time with other children.'
– *Lauren, primary school teacher and mother of two*

My grandmother looked after my children one day a week to help save the cost of placing them in nursery while I was studying. The benefit to me, apart from financial, was primarily peace of mind. I knew that my children were in a loving environment with someone who genuinely cared for them and with whom they felt comfortable. The benefits to my children were being able to spend time with their great-grandparents, forming bonds and making memories that they will continue to look back on fondly. My grandmother enjoyed being able to take part in the care of my children, experiencing them growing and learning, and sharing their laughter.'
– *Sally, student midwife and mother of two*

It's good to know that the person caring for your child genuinely loves them and is building a long-term, lifetime bond. It's also nice to think that the care will be as you experienced yourself as a child. At the outset I was very explicit about what was most important to me – no smacking, no shouting, and keeping the children safe, for example – so there could be no misunderstanding. I also provided the food and the environment. Reminding myself that I had that control helped me relax about the minor irritation of grandma giving too many cakes and biscuits! As the parent I think you need to be a little bit relaxed, especially if you're not paying for the care, and remember that it's OK if things are done differently, especially if it's just for a few hours a week.'
– *Sophie, social worker and mother of two*

'As a GP working long and unpredictable hours, grandparents have been an essential part of my childcare. I am completely relaxed at work knowing the kids are fine and I will get complete feedback about their day. If my children are ill, I don't have to take a day off. For a time, my parents would also have the children overnight when I did a late shift, which worked really well. It's important to have time to discuss how you manage situations and have a consistent approach. Good communication is vital, especially if you need different hours of help each week Although it's hard work, I think my parents love that they have been such an integral part of my children's lives. I give them gifts from time to time, but it struggles to compare with all the presents they have bought the children!'

– *Fiona, doctor and mother of two*

Chapter 7

Other types of childcare

An overview of your childcare choices if you don't need full daycare

The childcare options in this chapter won't be appropriate if you're looking for someone to care for a young child regularly while you work or study, but may suit you if you need childcare for other reasons.

Babysitters

There is no legal definition of a babysitter, but it's generally understood to be someone who cares for children (not just babies) in the family's home for a few hours in the evening while the parents are out.

Rates of pay are normally in the region of £5 to £10 an hour. It's usual to pay more for any hours after midnight or before 7pm, and on special occasions such as New Year's Eve. If your babysitter doesn't drive, offer to drive them home or pay for a taxi at the end of the evening. If you get home later than agreed, or have to cancel at short notice, give your babysitter an overtime or cancellation payment.

Families find babysitters in all sorts of ways. Often they are trusted neighbours, relatives or family friends whom the children already know well. Sometimes childminders, nannies, nursery staff or crèche workers are happy to earn extra money doing evening babysitting. Some parents find babysitters through private ads, online or in local papers or shop windows, in which case an interview, references and background checks are especially important. Others go through an agency, paying a premium for convenience and peace of mind.

However you find your babysitter, the NSPCC recommends that they should be no younger than 16. An under-16-year-old cannot be prosecuted for neglect or ill treatment of a child. Instead, as the child's parent, you would be held responsible should your child come to any harm.

Although there is no compulsory training, many parents like their babysitter to have completed a basic course in first aid for babies and children. The Red Cross and some other organisations offer training courses specifically in first aid for babysitters.

For babysitters employed through agencies, first aid training is usually standard, as is an enhanced Disclosure and Barring Service check (or equivalent). A good babysitting agency will also carry out interviews and reference checks, and may insist that all their babysitters have a childcare qualification or background. Parents usually have to pay a registration charge or regular membership fee to belong to the agency, as well as a booking fee each time they use one of their babysitters. Agencies that operate nationwide include Sitters (**www.sitters.co.uk**) and Safehands (**www.safehandsbabysitters.com**), and there are many more local ones.

A cost-free arrangement that works well for many families is to set up a babysitting circle, whereby a group of friends who all know each other's children agree to exchange babysitting services. Each member of the circle starts with a certain number of credits which are used to 'pay' for hours of babysitting from other group members. There are free services that will email babysitting requests to group members and manage everyone's credits too. Take a look at **www.babysittercircle.co.uk.**

Whoever is babysitting for you, there are a few bits of essential information they will need to know, so make a checklist covering:
- where you are going and what time you expect to be home
- mobile numbers for both parents
- an emergency contact – perhaps a neighbour or nearby friend
- full names and dates of birth of all children being babysat
- each child's bedtime and pre-sleep routine, including any comfort items such as a dummy or favourite soft toy
- any night-time habits (for example, a baby waking for a milk feed, or a child being prone to nightmares or sleepwalking)

- any allergies or medical conditions the children have, including medication the babysitter might need to give
- house rules, regarding smoking, having company or using the home phone, for example.

You should also show the babysitter around your home, so they know where each child sleeps and where they can relax after the little ones are in bed. Don't forget to cover:
- where to find babies' nappies and milk, and children's spare pyjamas and bedding
- emergency equipment such as the first aid kit, fire blanket/extinguisher and torch
- where the tea, coffee, soft drinks and snacks are
- how to work the TV, DVD player and broadband
- how to work the heating and any alarms
- how to deal with phone calls and personal callers.

It's a good idea to introduce your children to the babysitter before you go out, so if they wake in the night they don't find that their parents have been replaced by stranger! If the children are likely to be asleep before you leave, try to arrange for them to meet the babysitter beforehand.

You might also want to consider a baby monitor app for your phone or tablet, so that you can listen to, watch and even talk to your child while you are out. Dormi for Android devices and Cloud Baby Monitor for Apple are both highly rated, but there are many others.

Further information: **www.netmums.com** (search for 'babysitting').

Crèches*

Crèches offer short-term, occasional childcare, usually while children's parents are on the premises or nearby. They are commonly found in leisure centres, gyms and shopping centres, or where parents are attending a training course or conference. Crèches may be temporary or permanent, and may be set up to care for any age group, from babies as young as a few weeks to teenagers.

Crèches aren't required to register with Ofsted in England if parents remain on the premises and can be summoned immediately, and if care is provided for under four hours at a time, or less than five days a year, or only for children aged over eight – although a crèche in these circumstances may be on Ofsted's voluntary register. Crèches outside these parameters must be registered with Ofsted, and will need to meet most of the regulations that apply to nurseries (see page 39).

Charges are typically between £3 and £10 per child per hour, although many crèches are subsidised or even provided free. If you use a crèche that's Ofsted-registered, it may be possible to pay using childcare vouchers (see page 155).

The advantages of using a crèche – convenience and lack of a long-term commitment for you – may be disadvantages for your little one, as babies and young children often feel ill-at-ease being left in an unfamiliar environment with carers they don't know. If you plan to place a young child in a crèche, allow plenty of time to settle them before you leave.

You can get details of registered crèches in your area from your local Family Information Service, and in England check their inspection reports on the Ofsted website at **www.reports.ofsted.gov.uk**

Preschools

At preschools – sometimes referred to as playgroups, playschools or (confusingly) nurseries – children learn through play in a group setting. Many families find they provide a useful transition between home and 'big school', giving under-fives the opportunity to socialise and develop the skills and confidence they'll need in a reception class.

Preschools may be run privately, by a local authority, or on a voluntary basis – in which case parents often help out with running sessions, administration and fundraising. Some have permanent premises, but many operate from a church or village hall or community centre. Whatever the venue, there should be a range of educational activities and resources, and space for children to play outdoors as well as inside.

Preschools often accept children from age two or two-and-a-half, or when they are toilet trained. Community preschools/playgroups are generally cheaper than daycare nurseries and nursery schools. For children in England aged three and four, and some aged two, up to 15 (and soon 30) hours of preschool a week will be covered by their free early education entitlement – see page 159.

English preschools are registered and inspected by Ofsted and follow the Early Years Foundation Stage curriculum – see page 187 (equivalent inspection bodies and learning goals apply in other parts of the UK, as outlined on page 51). Staff ratios are the same as those in nurseries too.

Most preschools/playgroups operate fixed session times – usually mornings, but also sometimes afternoons or school-length days – during term-time only. Further information:
Pre-school Learning Alliance www.pre-school.org.uk

Out-of-school clubs*

Out-of-school clubs provide care for school-aged children before and after school and during school holidays. They may be referred to as breakfast clubs, after-school or homework clubs, and holiday clubs or playschemes. Opening hours for term-time clubs are usually 8am until school starts in the morning, and from school finishing time until 6pm. Holiday clubs are generally open all day, divided into a morning and afternoon session.

A good out-of-school club should provide a range of play equipment and activities, as well as opportunities for free play indoors and outside, and a quiet area where children can relax.

After-school and holiday clubs may offer lots of structured activities, such as crafts, group games, sports coaching, cookery, homework support, guest speakers or excursions. Some give children simple snacks, some offer a hot meal, and some expect parents to provide food.

State primary schools have to provide 'wraparound childcare' before and after school to support working parents, if there is sufficient demand. For this reason, term-time clubs are often based in or near schools, and some smaller schools walk or bus pupils to and from clubs at larger schools.

An out-of-school club may be managed by a school directly, the local authority, a specialist private company, a voluntary group or a local nursery. Whatever the arrangement, clubs in England must be registered and inspected by Ofsted, unless they cater solely for children aged over eight (in which case they may choose to register voluntarily). Rules around adult-child ratios for over-fives are less strict than in early years care, so check you are happy with the level of staffing and supervision.

Out-of-school club fees vary enormously – anything from £1 to £5 per child per hour is usual. The cost depends on whether the club receives any subsidy from the school or local authority, whether it's staffed by volunteers or paid workers, and the facilities and food on offer.

The advantages of an out-of-school club are that the care is normally convenient and affordable, and children are looked after alongside their classmates. Also, as out-of-school clubs are usually registered, you can take advantage of tax credits and tax-free childcare payment schemes (see chapter 9).

The downsides are the lack of choice – most schools provide just one childcare option, take it or leave it. The atmosphere can be hectic and overwhelming, which may not suit children who are very young, shy or tire easily. Also, if the club is school-based you may need to find alternative childcare in the school holidays.

You can get details of registered out-of-school clubs in your area from your local Family Information Service, and in England check out their inspection reports on the Ofsted website at **www.reports.ofsted.gov.uk** Further information: **www.outofschoolalliance.co.uk**

Mother's helps

A mother's help offers general assistance around the house, not just with childcare, while a parent is present. They may live in the family home or come daily, and can be full time or part time. A full-time mother's help normally works for around ten hours a day, five days a week.

A mother's help won't usually have a childcare qualification. They are often very young or newly arrived in the UK, interested in a childcare career and looking to gain experience. They may supervise and play with children and help with babycare, as well as doing light housework and chores, some food shopping and meal preparation, and running errands. They don't normally have sole charge of children during the day, except for very short periods (such as looking after a toddler while mum or dad does the school run), but they may do a couple of evenings' babysitting each week.

Recruiting a mother's help is much like hiring a nanny (see page 87). Gross full-time wages range from around £130 a week for a school-leaver or non-English, live-in mother's help, to £300 a week for a someone with excellent English who lives out and can drive. As mothers' helps are generally employed by the families they work for, you'll need to register as an employer with HMRC and submit payroll information if you pay your mother's help more than £112 a week, and pay employers' National Insurance if they earn over £155 (2016/17 figures).

Post-natal childcare

A professional post-natal childcarer can be a wonderful source of support in the often exhausting weeks after a baby is born. They will help to look after you and/or your baby while you recover from the birth and get to grips with feeding your newborn and establishing a sleep routine.

A post-natal childcarer may be particularly useful if you have a disability or chronic health condition, your partner and family can't provide much practical support, you have newborn twins (or more!), or you've had a caesarean or other birth complications.

There are three types of childcarer to choose from:

A maternity nurse is a nanny (not a qualified nurse) with training or experience in caring for newborns. They usually live with a family and are normally on duty 24 hours a day, six days a week. They have their own private room in the family home, which they normally share with the baby, so that parents can sleep with minimal interruptions. If the baby needs a night feed, the maternity nurse will take him or her to mum for a breastfeed, or give a bottle of expressed breastmilk or formula, and deal with winding and resettling afterwards. A maternity nurse handles all aspects of the baby's care, including nappy changes, bathing, dressing, the baby's laundry and keeping the nursery clean and tidy. They are not expected to do general housework, food preparation (the family provides all meals) or care for siblings. Their services generally cost between £100 and £200 per 24-hour day. If you have private health insurance, your policy may cover a maternity nurse in certain circumstances, such as if you have had a caesarean section or other birth complications.

A post-natal doula's role is 'mothering the mother'. They may help with caring for the baby, but will also do light housework, prepare meals and look after siblings if necessary, as well as giving the mother emotional support in recovering from the birth.

No formal qualifications are necessary to become a doula, but to be 'recognised' by the Doula UK network they must have attended a training course, been mentored by an experienced Doula and supported at least four families during or after the birth of a baby.

A post-natal doula normally comes to the family home for between four and eight hours a day, and charges between £12 and £25 per hour. Find out more at **www.doula.org.uk**.

A night nanny is a qualified nanny who will come to your home purely to help with night feeds, night-time babycare and establishing a sleep routine. They typically work a 10-hour shift from around 9pm until 7am, and charge from £80 to £150 a night. Parents often hire a night nanny for just two or three nights a week to help them catch up on sleep.

Post-natal childcarers are generally self-employed. Finding one is a similar process to hiring a nanny (see page 82) – through word-of-mouth, a private ad or an agency. As well as checking references, it's important to make sure you and the carer have a similar attitude and approach to babycare. If they're a queen of routine and you're a go-with-the-flow sort of parent (or vice versa), you may clash. You're likely to be feeling fragile, both physically and emotionally, after the birth, so you want a carer whose presence you'll find supportive and comforting, not intrusive or controlling.

Post-natal carers usually support a family for around six weeks, although you could engage one for just a fortnight or up to three months.

One tricky aspect of hiring a postnatal carer is that you don't know exactly when your baby will arrive, what the birth will be like, or how you'll feel afterwards. When interviewing candidates, discuss what will happen if your baby is premature or overdue, or if you or the baby have to stay in hospital.

Holiday childcare

If you're going on holiday as a family, you may need childcare while you're away. A little research and preparation before you travel will help you choose the best option for you and your child.

Some hotels provide a babysitting service, which normally means someone keeping watch over your child in your room while you go out. In the UK this is often (but not always) a trained and vetted childcare professional. Overseas it may not be, so check before you travel.

Other hotels offer a baby-listening service, which usually means a member of staff listening in to your room phone (and those of other parents using the service) and alerting you if they hear any crying or disturbance. It's worth asking a few questions before using a listening service: Who will be listening, and how frequently? Could staff enter your room while you're not there? Could your child get out into a corridor or on to a balcony? What happens if the fire alarm goes off?

Some parents use their own baby monitors or a baby monitor phone app, or a set of walkie-talkies, to listen in to their hotel room while they dine or attend a function on-site (although none of these resolves security and fire issues). Another possibility, especially if you are holidaying in the UK, is to book an agency babysitter – with the hotel's agreement of course. This may be less expensive than a hotel babysitting service and more reassuring than a listening service, and may broaden your choice of hotels. It's also an option if you are on a self-catering holiday.

If you are staying in a UK hotel or holiday resort with a crèche or kids' club, these will have to meet exactly the same standards as other crèches and kids' clubs in that part of the UK. You should be able to find the Ofsted (or equivalent) inspection report online.

Overseas the quality of holiday childcare varies hugely. If being able to leave your child in a crèche or kids' club is an important part of your holiday plans, check out the childcare provision before you book. In particular, are staff trained or qualified, and what's the ratio of adults to children? Large UK tour operators are increasingly striving to meet UK standards in their holiday childcare settings, but this may not be the case for smaller or foreign companies. Check staff ratios against those for nurseries on page 40.

Before leaving your child in a holiday crèche or kids' club, check that the equipment and environment seem safe and secure, and that bathrooms, changing areas, and arrangements for food preparation are hygienic. Ask questions, just as you would when leaving your child with a carer in the UK. Is there a keyworker system? Do all staff speak English? What records do you keep? What activities are provided? What are the arrangements for meals and snacks? What plans are there for emergencies? Make sure staff have mobile numbers for you and other adults in your party so they can contact you quickly if need be.

If you have niggling doubts about any holiday childcare provision, steer clear. Don't compromise your standards because you're away from home. Further information:
www.babycentre.co.uk/a561721/how-to-find-good-childcare-on-holiday

The information about registration of crèches and out-of-school clubs in this chapter applies to England only; different rules apply elsewhere in the UK. In Wales these forms of care are registered and inspected by the Care and Social Services Inspectorate Wales; in Scotland by the Care Inspectorate; and in Northern Ireland by local health and social care trusts.

Chapter 8

Childcare for children with additional needs

Finding and funding childcare for youngsters who need extra support

If your child has additional needs of any sort – whether a physical impairment, chronic medical condition, learning difficulties, behavioural issues, communication problems or severe allergies – you'll want to be sure that the childcare you choose gives them the support they require.

Finding the right childcare for a child with additional needs may take extra time, initiative and determination on your part, but it's well worth the effort. All children need opportunities to play, learn and make friends, and all parents should have access to good quality, affordable childcare to allow them to work or study.

Every local authority in England, as well as each individual nursery and Sure Start centre, must have a Special Educational Needs Coordinator (Senco). Their role is to work with you and your child, as well as staff and outside agencies, to make sure your son or daughter gets appropriate support to meet their additional needs. In many local authorities the Senco is part of a specialist staff team helping childcare and early years education providers deliver an inclusive service.

If your child has any sort of additional needs, it's a good idea to make contact with your local authority's Senco as early as possible. They should be able to tell you about the childcare options available to you, as well as any funding you might be entitled to. They will also give advice about inclusion, making sure your child has equal access to play and learning opportunities and that you and your family are welcomed and respected in childcare settings, as well as identifying and removing any barriers to accessing quality childcare, and giving you the knowledge and power to make informed decisions.

Think about the practicalities of what your child needs, and discuss with the Senco what you might reasonably ask a childcare provider to offer. Information about inclusion funding, details of grants available for settings, and help for childcare providers to get relevant training are examples of the support a Senco might provide.

Your local authority's Family Information Service should also be able to give you information about childcare provision for children with additional needs in your area.

Did you know?

Local Authorities in England have to publish details of the provision they expect to be available for children with special educational needs and disabilities in their 'Local Offer'. This must include childcare provision and must appear on their website. The Local Offer was introduced as part of the Children and Families Act which came into force in September 2014.

Your rights

It's good to know that the law is on your side. Local authorities in England have a duty to ensure there is suitable childcare accessible to all families who need it (under the Childcare Act 2006) – and this duty covers disabled children up to the age of 18. Also, childcarers are not allowed to treat a disabled child less favourably than any other child (to comply with the Equality Act 2010), and must make 'reasonable adjustments' to accommodate youngsters with additional needs.

Making reasonable adjustments should be a partnership between your family and the childcare provider. Childcarers and local authorities put themselves at risk of breaking the law by not considering reasonable adjustments or providing support to include children with additional needs in mainstream childcare settings.

A reasonable adjustment could be almost anything. Examples include:
- repositioning furniture, and moving toys and equipment so that all children have access to all the playthings and activities on offer
- adapting activities and excursions so that all children can participate
- introducing new policies and procedures – for example a 'no nuts' policy and different catering arrangements to accommodate a child with a severe nut allergy
- specialist training for staff, in Makaton sign language or giving insulin injections, for instance
- extra equipment or resources, such as a Braille computer keyboard, audio induction hearing loop, large-type books, or a separate fridge for medicines
- additional staff, for children who need one-to-one attention all or some of the time
- modifications to the building, such as adding access ramps, grab-rails or a disabled parking bay
- accommodating specialist services providers, such as speech therapists or physiotherapists, within the childcare setting.

What's classed as 'reasonable' depends on the setting and is decided on a case-by-case basis. Childcarers may be able to get grants and practical support to help them make adjustments. Again, your local authority's Senco should be able to provide more information.

Specialist childcare

Many local authorities have funding available to support the inclusion of children in mainstream settings whose needs cannot be met through reasonable adjustments. This might cover:
- personal assistants for intensive support and one-to-one care
- training for staff in specialist skills such as manual handling administering medicines or alternative communication methods
- funding for adjustments to the physical environment.

What's available depends on the local authority and the individual child's level of need.

If your child's needs can't be accommodated in a mainstream setting, you might want to consider a specialist childcare provider.

Your local authority Senco or Family Information Service should be able to tell you about any local nurseries and playschemes specifically for disabled children, as well as about specially trained registered childminders, and home childcarers if your child needs care in their own home.

There are also private nanny agencies that specialise in providing families with childcarers who have training or experience in caring for disabled children and those with special educational needs. Snap Childcare (**www.snapchildcare.co.uk**) is one that covers the whole of the UK, and a web search may reveal others in your area.

Did you know?
In England, if your child has an Education, Health and Care Plan, or a Statement of Special Educational Needs, or if you claim Disability Living Allowance for them (or anyone else does), they are eligible for fifteen free hours of early education each week during term time after they turn two. You don't need to be working or studying to access this. (See page 160 for more information.)

Financial support

As well as the financial help available to all parents with children in childcare (see chapter 9), you may be entitled to extra support if your child has additional needs. In particular you should check your entitlement to tax credits (see page 153), as the amount you receive may be higher if your child is eligible for Disability Living Allowance or is registered blind.

If your child has significant additional needs and has been given an Education, Health and Care Plan, you might be able to get money from your local authority to pay for care – including childcare – with the care provider of your choice under the 'Direct Payments' system. Find out more at: **www.cafamily.org.uk** (search for 'direct payments')

It's well worth speaking to a specialist advisor to make sure you and your child are getting all the financial support you're entitled to. Try Citizen's Advice: **www.citizensadvice.org.uk**, or call 03444 111444 (in England) or Contact a Family's benefits advice line: **www.cafamily.org.uk/know-your-rights/benefits-and-tax-credits** or call free on 0808 808 3555.

The reality of finding childcare for children with additional needs

Despite the practical help, legal protections and financial assistance in place, many parents of children with additional needs still struggle to find suitable childcare.

A parliamentary enquiry in 2014 found that in 72 per cent of families with a disabled child, one or both parents had cut back on or given up paid work because of childcare difficulties. The vast majority (86 per cent) said they were paying an above-average rate for their childcare, and a massive 92 per cent thought that finding childcare for a disabled child was more difficult than for a non-disabled child.

The same research discovered that three-quarters of local authorities didn't have enough childcare provision for disabled children, and 41 per cent of families couldn't access the full amount of free early years education their child was entitled to.

It seems that, for many families, the problems get worse as their child gets older. After all, most childcarers are used to dealing with children who aren't mobile, can't communicate clearly, aren't toilet-trained and need a special diet – when the children in question are babies. It's continuing to accommodate these needs as a child grows, while ensuring they can enjoy the same play and learning opportunities as their peers, that some settings struggle with. Many parents also face practical problems, such as finding childcare that fits around disabled children's medical appointments and hospitalisations, and which accommodates non-disabled siblings too.

Emerging special needs

Sometimes a child's additional needs may not be apparent when they start childcare, but might emerge later on. In England, all compulsorily registered early years providers (ie nurseries, childminders, and preschools) must follow the Early Years Foundation Stage framework (see page 188), which requires them to monitor children's learning, development and wellbeing against national guidelines. If your childcarer is concerned that your child's development may be outside the norms for their age, whether physically, socially, behaviourally, emotionally or academically, they will raise this with you.

The EYFS requires early years professionals to identify and respond to young children's special educational needs, as early intervention gives youngsters the best long-term outcomes. The childcarer (or special educational needs co-ordinator – Senco – in centre-based care) will discuss with you and your child what additional help may be needed, and the three of you will work together to develop an action plan, which could include information about:

- short-term learning targets for your child
- special help to be given, by whom, and how often
- support from outside experts, such as a speech therapist or Portage worker (a specialist who works with preschool children who have additional needs and their families, usually in the home)
- how and when your child's progress will be checked
- resources that might benefit your child
- suggestions of assistance you can give your child at home.

This approach is called SEN Support.

Often, the targeted help provided by SEN Support will help your child to catch up with their peers. However, if your child has complex needs that will continue to have an impact on their education, health and care as they grow up, they may need a Education, Health and Care plan (EHC). EHCs replaced Statements of Special Educational Needs in 2014. They help to ensure that children with additional needs have access to appropriate extra support, resources and services at school age and beyond.

Making a complaint

Unfortunately, it's all too common that families with disabled children experience stigma and discrimination when trying to arrange childcare. If you need to make a complaint or want support resolving issues around a childcare provider's lack of reasonable adjustments, contact your local authority. In England, information about making a complaint should be contained in their Local Offer.

Further information

These organisations offer support and advice to parents of children with additional needs, including information about childcare.

Contact a Family
www.cafamily.org.uk

Council for Disabled Children
www.councilfordisabledchildren.org.uk

Family and Childcare Trust
www.familyandchildcaretrust.org/childcare

Independent Advice and Support Services network
www.iassnetwork.org.uk

National Children's Bureau
www.ncb.org.uk/areas-of-activity/sen-and-disability

National Network of Parent Carer Forums
www.nnpcf.org.uk

Working Families
www.workingfamilies.org.uk

Around the UK

The information in this chapter refers primarily to children with additional needs in England. Wales, Scotland and Northern Ireland have different childcare laws, and different equality legislation applies in Northern Ireland too.

If you live outside England, try contacting one of the following organisations for advice and support:

Wales

Children in Wales: **www.childreninwales.org.uk**

Snap Cymru: **www.snapcymru.org**

Scotland

For Scotland's Disabled Children: **www.fsdc.org.uk**

Capability Scotland – Childcare for All:

www.capability-scotland.org.uk (search for 'childcare')

Northern Ireland

Special Educational Needs Advice Centre: **www.senac.co.uk**

NI Direct: **www.nidirect.gov.uk/caring-for-a-child-with-disabilities**

What parents say...

My son went to a daycare nursery full time from the age of nine months. I felt that it would be easier to get help from outside agencies if we used centre-based care, and liked the idea of there being more people to look out for him. I got a good feel from the nursery from the moment we first went to see it, and they were really supportive throughout his years there. We were already accessing Portage through the local authority, and the Portage team would go to the nursery to give advice to the staff, for example on toys to build up his strength. My son's fantastic physiotherapist also went in, and the occupational therapy service sent a specialist too. We all learned together as he grew and developed. My advice to other parents is to engage as many specialist professionals as possible and get their perspective and opinion before choosing a childcare or education setting. In our case, I always felt that mainstream provision was the best choice. I think that with children who have special needs of any kind, the more you can socialise them the better. And it's so important for other children to be aware of those with additional needs. Your child has every right to good quality childcare and education. Go with your gut instinct regarding what's best for your child. Fight for what you want, and then work as a team with the staff and specialists. Now, aged eight, my son has strong speech and is a very sociable child thriving in a mainstream school. I'm sure attending a mainstream nursery helped him.'
– *Sarah, IT contracts manager and mother of three*

I chose a childminder for my son, originally due to him being profoundly deaf in one ear. As he's still so young it seemed better for him to be in a quieter environment with one carer, to give him more time and attention if he struggled with speech or communication. It's so important his speech is nurtured at this early stage. Now, due to his allergies and tube-feeding, I am even more sure it's the right decision as he can be more closely supervised. I can more easily provide food for him and there will only be one carer doing his feeds. My childminder is being trained in tube feeding and has also done lots of investigations into what she needs to have in place to provide care for him. I trust that she will minimise risk for him as much as possible and meet his needs well.'

– *Nicola, social worker and mother of three*

Because R couldn't walk, a lot of nurseries wanted to put him with younger children, but I was determined he should be with his peer group. Eventually we found a nursery that was very encompassing and welcoming. They made adjustments so that R could enjoy free-flow play while "bottom-shuffling", and worked with the local authority's inclusion support team to get the one-to-one adult support and extra equipment he needed. Because of his disability, we got funding for R to go to nursery from the age of two. It's benefited him so much. He really needed the social development, learning how to interact and communicate with other children his age. Being at home with me and his sister just wasn't giving him enough stimulation. Nursery gives him more opportunities and space to play and learn new skills. He loves going, and is very settled there.'

– *Catherine, full-time mother of two*

Chapter 9

Paying for childcare

Schemes to help make childcare more affordable, whether you're working or studying

As well as giving careful thought to the type of childcare you're going to use, it's worth considering just as carefully how you're going to pay for it. Childcare costs can be a big drain on the family finances, so make the most of any support you might be entitled to. There's help available, whether you're a schoolgirl mum or a highflying professional earning over £100,000 a year.

The cost of childcare often comes as a huge shock to new parents. For many families it can be like taking on a second mortgage. In fact the Families and Childcare Trust's Annual Childcare Costs Study 2014 found that the average UK family with two children, one attending a daycare nursery part-time and one in an after-school club, paid £7,549 a year for their childcare, compared with £7,207 for their mortgage.

British parents spend a higher proportion of their salaries on childcare than their counterparts in all other European countries except Switzerland, according to a 2012 report from the Organisation for Economic Co-operation and Development (OECD). And the problem of affordability has worsened in recent years. Between 2009 and 2014, childcare costs rose by an average of 27 per cent (Family and Childcare Trust figures), while incomes fell in real terms.

Yet childcare remains a poorly paid and undervalued profession. People are often prepared to pay more per hour for someone to do their cleaning or ironing than to look after their child, even though most would agree that caring for a child is a vastly more demanding and responsible job. According to the Low Pay Commission, from 2012–14 average pay across the childcare workforce (excluding nannies) was just £6.60 an hour or £10,324 a year.

So, value your childcare provider for the vital work they do, and pay them properly by making the most of the various schemes on offer to help with childcare costs.

The childcare element of Working Tax Credit

The childcare element of Working Tax Credit helps cover childcare fees for lower income working families who use registered or approved childcare. To be eligible, you must be a single parent working at least 16 hours a week, or part of a couple where both parents work at least 16 hours a week (or one partner is unable to work or care for children for some reason). You can be working for yourself or employed by someone else.

The childcare element covers up to 70 per cent of your childcare fees, up to a maximum weekly childcare cost of £175 for one child and £300 for two or more children (so you could receive up to £122.50 or £210 respectively).

You will qualify for these maximum payments only if you are on a very low household income of £6,420 a year or less. If your earnings are is higher you may still be eligible for a reduced payment. The rules are complex, but it's definitely worth checking your entitlement if your household income is under £45,000 (or possibly higher if you have several children in paid childcare and/or anyone in your family is disabled).

The money is normally paid directly into your bank or building society account, but can also be offset against your tax liability. You can claim until the September following your child's 15th birthday (or 16th birthday if they're disabled).

The best way to find out if you qualify is to call the Tax Credits Helpline on 0345 300 3900 (weekdays 8am until 8pm or Saturdays until 4pm). You can also get an estimate of the amount of money you may receive using the online Tax Credits Calculator at:

www.gov.uk/tax-credits-calculator

Find out more about Working Tax Credit, and the childcare element in particular, at: **www.hmrc.gov.uk/leaflets/wtc5.pdf** and **www.gov.uk/childcare-tax-credits**

Did you know?

Working Tax Credit, including the childcare element, is being absorbed into the Government's new Universal Credit (UC) system, which is already up and running in some parts of the country and is gradually being rolled out to families across the UK. For parents claiming the childcare costs element of UC there is no minimum limit to the number of hours you have to work, and the maximum childcare cost that's eligible has increased to £532.29 a month for one child or £912.50 per month for two or more children. The maximum proportion of childcare costs you can claim for under Universal Credit is 85 per cent, compared with 70 per cent under Working Tax Credit.

There have, however, been criticisms of UC. Some working parents who currently receive Housing Benefit and Council Tax Benefit may be worse off under the new system, with those who have large families or who live in high-cost housing areas most likely to be affected. UC is also means-tested, so any capital you have (such as savings, lump sums or some types of property) over £6,000 will reduce the amount you receive.

Read more about Universal Credit at:

www.gov.uk/universal-credit

What parents say...

'We weren't eligible for Working Families' Tax Credit when we had just one child, but we are now that we have two. The amount we get is a little higher because our son has a disability.'
– *Catherine, full-time mother of two*

'I have been claiming Working Families' Tax Credit for childcare since my son was eight months old. I found claiming very easy initially, and it was also straightforward when changing my childcare provider from nursery to after-school/holiday care. Working Families' Tax Credit has been a godsend, as without it there's no way I could have afforded to have gone back to work as childcare costs are so expensive. Although the childcare element does not cover the full childcare cost, the rest of the Child/Working Tax Credits I get helps cover that and also gives me a little extra on top of my monthly wage for food, rent and general living costs. I have on a few occasions made changes and found it's sorted really easily by a phone call.'
– *Trudy, production operative and mother of one*

Employer-supported childcare vouchers

If you're employed, childcare vouchers from your employer could be a big help in paying for childcare.

All sorts of employers, large and small, offer their staff childcare vouchers. This is normally done as part of a salary sacrifice arrangement, which means you give up part of your gross salary to pay for the vouchers. In return, you pay no income tax on this money, and neither you nor your employer pay National Insurance contributions (NICs) on it.

The maximum amount of gross salary you can use to pay for childcare

vouchers is currently:
- £55 a week if you're a basic rate taxpayer
- £28 a week if you're a higher rate taxpayer
- £25 a week if you're an additional rate taxpayer.

Until April 2011, all employees were entitled to the £55 a week rate, so if you entered your company's childcare vouchers scheme before this date you can continue to claim this amount, no matter what level of income tax you pay. You will lose this entitlement once you leave your company or your child turns 15, whichever comes sooner.

The savings on tax and National Insurance are typically worth around £933 a year for a basic rate taxpayer. As both parents can claim vouchers, if you and your partner are both in work, your family could be almost £1,900 a year better off than if you paid for childcare from your net income.

To be eligible for childcare vouchers, you must have a child under the age of 15 (or 16 if they're disabled) in childcare that's registered or approved by Ofsted in England (or other regulatory bodies in other parts of the UK). In practice this means almost all daycare nurseries, pre-schools, nursery schools or classes, and after-school and holiday clubs, most childminders, many nannies, a few au pairs, and even some private tutors, as well as private schools until the term before your child's fifth birthday. Do check that your provider accepts vouchers before signing up to your company's scheme.Childcare vouchers cannot be used to pay for family childcare unless the family member who looks after your child is a registered childminder also available to care for other children.

An employer may run their own voucher scheme, or operate one through a specialist voucher provider (there are almost 20 nationwide). In either case, the vouchers may be paper coupons that you give to your childcare provider instead of cash, or they may be paid electronically into a special account for you to transfer to your childcarer's bank account.

You can normally sign up to your company's childcare vouchers scheme as soon as your baby is born, so you and/or your partner could build up a stock of vouchers while you are on parental leave to help pay for childcare once you return to work. Some companies will also allow you to accrue them during any subsequent spells of maternity or paternity leave, even if you don't use paid-for childcare during this time.

Paper vouchers often expire after a year, while electronic ones are less likely to have a time limit – but it's worth checking the exact rules of your company's scheme. You'll also want to find out what happens to any unused vouchers if you leave your company or end your childcare arrangement. Sometimes you can get the cash back (after paying tax and NICs on it, of course), but some vouchers are not refundable or transferable.

You will probably need to sign a declaration agreeing to give up part of your salary in return for the vouchers. Bear in mind that, although your will save on childcare costs, the salary sacrifice will make your gross income lower for as long as you are part of the voucher scheme. This could have an impact on any salary-related benefits or calculations. For example, it could affect pension or mortgage calculations, or reduce your maternity pay if you have another baby. Paying for childcare with vouchers could also reduce the amount of Working Tax Credit you are entitled to. If you are not sure whether it will be financially worthwhile joining your employer's voucher scheme, try using the HMRC 'better-off calculator':

www.hmrc.gov.uk/calcs/ccin.htm

Alternatively you could speak to an advisor at your Citizens Advice Bureau, Sure Start centre or Job Centre.

Find out whether your employer has a childcare voucher scheme and, if so, how it works, by talking to your HR or Personnel department. If there isn't already a scheme in place, encourage them to set one up (after all, it should save them money!) They must do this by April 2018, as the rules around tax-free childcare are changing (See page 159).

For more information about employer-supported childcare vouchers go to:

www.hmrc.gov.uk/leaflets/ir115.pdf
www.moneysavingexpert.com/family/childcare-vouchers

> **What parents say...**

My wife and I both receive childcare vouchers from our employers. The vouchers have helped to cover the growing costs of childcare for our children. The nursery fees for my daughter alone are now £1,350 a month – crazy!'
– Joe, IT project manager and father of three

I kept claiming vouchers and storing them up while I was on maternity leave for the second time. They were a huge help when I eventually went back to work and had to cover the cost of childcare for two children.'
–Beth, journalist and mother of two

I work for a small building contractors. When we had our little girl, I asked my colleague in Finance to set up the childcare voucher scheme, and she did it no problem. Then all the other dads I work with got in on the act, and wondered why they'd never done it before!'
– Brett, carpenter and father of one

Other sorts of employer-supported childcare

Directly contracted childcare

Some companies pay a local nursery, crèche, after-school club, registered childminder or approved nanny to provide care for employees' children. This is called 'directly contracted childcare', and the same limits apply as for childcare vouchers, meaning your employer can pay the childcarer up to the amounts given on page 156 and you won't have to pay tax or NICS on this sum. However, if your employer pays your childcarer anything over these limits, you will have to pay tax and NICS on the additional amount.

Workplace nurseries

If you're lucky enough to work for an employer who provides and funds a workplace nursery, you do not have to pay tax or NICs on this benefit. Read more about workplace nurseries at:

http://vouchers.employersforchildcare.org/media/workplace-nurseries-1.pdf

The tax-free childcare scheme

Under the tax-free childcare scheme, from early 2017, for every 80p parents pay towards childcare the Government will add 20p (the equivalent of the basic-rate income tax payable on that amount).

The maximum amount the Government will contribute is £2000 per child per year (ie to help with childcare costs of up to £10,000 a year), with no limit on the number of children that can be claimed for in each family. The scheme is for working single parents and couples who use childcare registered or approved by Ofsted in England (or other regulatory bodies in other parts of the UK) for children aged up to 12 (and disabled children aged up to 17).

Unlike the childcare vouchers system, this alternative scheme allows self-employed people and those whose companies do not provide vouchers to benefit from tax-free childcare. It is for all working parents who earn up to £150,000 individually, except those who receive Tax Credits or Universal Credit (as their childcare costs are supported by the childcare element of these benefits).

To participate, parents must open a special childcare account through the **www.gov.uk** website. Both parents, and anyone else who wants to contribute towards the family's childcare costs, can pay into the account. Each family will have just one account (unlike childcare vouchers, where two working parents could each have an account).

One controversial aspect of the scheme is that couples where one partner has chosen to be a stay-at-home parent are not eligible. Both partners must work at least eight hours a week and have a minimum weekly income averaging just over £50 to qualify.

Find out more about tax-free childcare from 2017 at:
www.gov.uk/government/news/
tax-free-childcare-10-things-parents-should-know

Free early education

All three- and four-year-olds in England are entitled to 570 hours of free early education a year. Your child could receive this from one or more of the following providers, depending on your preference and availability in your area:

Daycare nursery – usually open most of the year, from at least 8am until 6pm, and managed by a trained nursery nurse. (See chapter 2 for more information.)

Nursery school or **nursery class** – usually open for set sessions, term-time only, with a trained teacher in charge. Often attached to a state or private school, with perhaps more formal learning than in a daycare nursery or preschool.

Preschool (sometimes known as a **playgroup**) – usually open for set sessions, term-time only. Often run on a not-for-profit basis, with trained and volunteer staff working under a nursery nurse leader (see page 131).

Sure Start centre – local authority provision, which may be run along similar lines to a daycare nursery, nursery school or preschool.

Registered childminder – some childminders deliver funded early education in a home setting.

All of these settings are registered and inspected by Ofsted, and whichever one your child attends they will be following the same curriculum – the Early Years Foundation Stage framework (see page 188).

Your child can access their free education from the start of the term following their third birthday, so those born from January to March get it after Easter, those born from April to August receive it from September, and those born from September to December qualify from January.

Free early education is also now available to some two-year-olds from the term following their second birthday. To qualify, you must be receiving a benefit such as Income Support, Jobseeker's Allowance or Working Tax Credit, and have a household income below £16,190 a year. All two-year-olds with an Education, Health and Care Plan, or for whom someone claims Disability Living Allowance, are also eligible.

The 570 hours are normally taken as 15 hours a week during term time, although some settings may offer 'stretched' provision – for example twelve hours a week for 48 weeks a year.

Did you know...

The Government is extending the free entitlement in England to 30 hours a week during term time (or equivalent) for three- and four-year-olds who have both parents (or a single parent) working at least sixteen hours a week and not earning more than £100,000 each. This is being be piloted in eight local authorities from autumn 2016, and rolled out across England from September 2017.

If your toddler is already in childcare, you may be able to use their early education funding to pay their existing care provider once they turn three (or two if they're eligible), significantly reducing your childcare costs. Alternatively, if your toddler has been with a home-based child-carer such as a childminder, nanny or grandparents, you could reduce their hours (and your costs) with this carer and use the free hours to let your child experience a group setting before they start school.

You do not have to claim early education funding as a parent. You simply fill in a form that your provider gives you and they will claim on your child's behalf. Government guidance states that providers should not charge parents any 'top-up' payment on top of the free entitlement. In practice, however, some providers find that the funding doesn't cover their costs and so charge for 'extras', such as compulsory additional hours, a lunch club, or a registration fee. Make sure you are clear about any additional fees, and how and when they are payable, when you put your child's name down with any early education provider.

Even if your child is just a baby when you return to work or study, it's worth thinking about how you might use their free early education entitlement once they turn three (or two). It's something you might want to include in your list of interview questions when choosing childcare. Find out more about free early education in England at:

www.gov.uk/free-early-education
www.foundationyears.org.uk/early-education-entitlement/

Early education around the UK

Rules regarding free early education in other parts of the UK vary...

Children aged three or four living in Wales are entitled to at least ten hours of early education each week. It's up to individual local authorities to deliver this, so rules covering exactly how many hours your preschooler can have, and who can provide them, depend on where you live. In practice, children normally receive two or two and a half hours of funded education each weekday during term time. To find out about early education in your area, contact your local authority's Family Information Service or education department.

Under the Flying Start scheme, two- and three-year-olds from disadvantaged backgrounds in Wales can also receive two and a half hours a day of early education during term time. Read more about this at: **www.gov.wales** (search for 'flying start')

In Scotland, children aged three and four, and some aged two, are entitled to 600 hours of funded early learning and childcare a year, which local authorities should administer flexibly to meet parents' needs. Find out more at: **www.scottishfamilies.gov.uk**

In Northern Ireland, children are entitled to at least a year of free early education before they start school, normally delivered as two and a half hours a day, five days a week, during term time. Unlike in England, it's the responsibility of the parent, not the education provider, to apply for the funding: **www.nidirect.gov.uk/articles/funded-pre-school-education**

Help with childcare if you're a student

If you're a student, you may be able to get financial support from the Government or from your college or university to help cover your childcare costs while you study. As well as the hourly or daily rate you pay your childcare provider, your childcare costs could include a deposit, registration fee, retainer fee or additional travel. Whether you qualify for any childcare support, and how much you might get, depends on a wide range of factors, including the type of course you're doing, whether it's full- or part-time, how old you are, where you're studying, how many children you have, how old they are, your household income, whether you receive any benefits, and more.

The National Union of Students provides a comprehensive overview: www.nus.org.uk/childcare

Subsidised nursery place

Many colleges and universities have their own on-site nursery, and fees may be subsidised for students' children. To find out about childcare provision at your place of learning consult the prospectus or website, or contact the student office.

Student Childcare Grant

If you're a full-time student and you have at least one child aged under 15 (or under 17 if they're disabled or have special educational needs), you may be able to claim a Student Childcare Grant. This will cover up to 85 per cent of your childcare costs while you study. The maximum you can receive is £155.24 a week for one child and up to £266.15 a week for two or more children (2016/17 figures).

Find out more at:
www.gov.uk/childcare-grant

Care to Learn

If you're a parent aged 20 or under, the Care to Learn scheme could help with childcare if you're studying at a publicly funded institution, such as a school, sixth form college or FE college. (Students in higher education and apprentices are not eligible.) To qualify for Care to Learn funding, you must be using registered childcare, such as a daycare nursery or childminder. The money is paid directly to your childcare provider, and covers childcare costs of up to £160 per child per week (or £175 per child per week in London), as well as extras such as deposits, retainer fees, settling-in sessions, holiday care, and additional travel necessary for your childcare arrangement.

Find out more about Care to Learn and get an application form from: www.gov.uk/care-to-learn/overview

Parents' Learning Allowance

Full-time students who have dependent children may be eligible for Parents' Learning Allowance (worth up to £1,573 in 2016/17). This is on top of any other student finance you may be entitled to, and doesn't have to be spent on childcare – so you could use it to pay for transport, books, learning materials, or anything else to support your studies. The money is normally paid termly, and how much you receive depends on your household income and other factors. You should apply for Parents' Learning Allowance at the same time as applying for Student Finance.

www.gov.uk/parents-learning-allowance/overview
www.thestudentroom.co.uk

Discretionary Learner Support

If you're aged 20 or over and facing financial hardship, you may be able to claim Discretionary Learner Support (DLS) to help cover your childcare costs. Every college and university has its own DLS scheme, so whether you're eligible and how much you might receive will depend on the rules at your particular institution. Ask at your student office for full details.

NHS Dependants' Allowance and Childcare Allowance

If you're a student of medicine, dentistry, nursing or certain other health-care professions in England, and you receive an NHS bursary, you may be eligible for NHS Dependants' Allowance or Childcare Allowance.

Find out more at **www.gov.uk/nhs-bursaries/further-information.**

Student childcare support around the UK

Some of the childcare support on offer to students is slightly different in other parts of the UK. Use the following websites to check what you might be entitled to:

Wales: www.studentfinancewales.co.uk (search for 'childcare')

Scotland: www.saas.gov.uk (search for 'childcare')

Northern Ireland: www.studentfinanceni.co.uk (click 'I am a student with children')

What parents say...

'I got Care to Learn. If you're in full-time education and under 20 it pays your full-time childcare costs while you study. There are tough conditions: you have to attend full time, any time you don't attend you get the nursery bill for that day, and if your attendance drops below about 90 per cent they can cut you off completely. It was a good scheme that got me through three years of college as a teen mum, and I'm now fully qualified.'
– *Katie, hairdresser and mother of two*

'I did manage to get Student Childcare Grant, but the rules around household income, savings and so on are very strict and I found the forms a pain to complete. It's worth speaking to an advisor to check whether you're eligible before attempting to apply.'
– *Naima, nurse and mother of one*

Further information about help with paying for childcare
www.moneyadviceservice.org.uk/en/articles/
help-with-childcare-costs
www.moneysavingexpert.com/family/childcare-costs
www.pacey.org.uk/parents/paying_for_childcare.aspx

Chapter 10

Making it work

How to make your chosen childcare arrangement a success for you, your family and your care provider

You've chosen a childcarer. Congratulations! Now it's time to think about settling your child, developing a good relationship with your care provider, and the practicalities of being a working or studying parent.

Preparing your child for childcare

There are lots of things you can do with your child to help get them ready for starting childcare. It's not fair on your child or childcarer if the first day of daycare is the first time your little one has been apart from mum, encountered older children, or had to eat or sleep an unfamiliar place. Attending toddler groups together will get your son or daughter used to being around other adults and interacting with other children. Leaving them with another family member or friend sometimes, including for meals and naps, will help them become accustomed to being apart from you. If you practise attachment parenting, think about how you will manage your baby's transition to childcare, and discuss it with your childcarer in advance.

Talk to your child about childcare, especially if you regularly pass their eventual nursery or childminder's house, or they have friends or family already in daycare. Once you have chosen a care-provider, you might want to take photos of your child's carer or key worker, the setting and any favourite things – such as a playhouse, climbing frame, pets or musical instruments – to talk about later.

Always try to keep your tone light and positive during conversations about childcare. Even if you're feeling anxious or daunted about the prospect of leaving your child, you don't want them to pick up on this. If you know any other families who use the same childcare setting, you could arrange a playdate before your child starts there. As well as being a chance for the little ones to get to know one another, it's a good opportunity for you to get the lowdown from another parent who uses the service. See if you can attend any family events that the childcare provider might be holding in the run-up to your child's start date, such as a summer fête, Christmas party, charity fundraiser or parents' coffee morning. It's a good idea to try to get into the pattern of a childcare day before the arrangement

Useful books

You might want to read some relevant picture books with your child. Titles written to help young children understand daycare, having working parents and spending time apart from family include:

Ladybird Toddler Touch: Nursery
(aimed at babies and young toddlers)

I'm Starting Nursery by Amanda Li

Maisy Goes to Nursery by Lucy Cousins

Owl Babies by Martin Waddell

Who Will Sing my Puff-a-Bye? by Charlotte Hudson
(aimed at children being cared for by a childminder or nanny)

Mummy Goes to Work by Kes Gray

The Kissing Hand by Audrey Penn

Mama Always Comes Home by Karma Wilson

starts, so that the whole family gets used to waking up, having meals and snacks, and going to bed, at the times they will on childcare days. You'll probably want to rehearse the morning routine too, so that by the time your first day back at work or college comes around you're confident about getting everyone up, dressed, breakfasted, to the childcarer, and to your place of work or study on time during the morning rush-hour.

If your child is being cared for away from home, label everything! These days it's not a case of laboriously sewing in name tags. You can buy inexpensive, wash-proof adhesive or iron-on name labels for clothes, and dishwashable, microwaveable vinyl labels for lunchboxes, baby bottles and other equipment.

Settling in

All experienced childcare professionals will have tried and tested ways of settling young children into their care, so take their advice and be guided by them in the early days.

Childcare providers usually offer a settling-in period to get your little one used to their new care arrangement. A gradual introduction over two to four weeks is ideal, but some settings offer as little as two hours. Settling-in sessions may be free or charged at the standard rate. Your contract and any record forms should be completed before you leave your child for the first time.

A settling-in period will normally begin with you and your child attending the childcare setting together for a short while – perhaps half an hour. During the next visit, you leave for a few minutes. Then you build up to longer visits and longer spells with no parent present, until you all feel ready for the contractual childcare arrangement to begin.

Many childcarers will ask you to complete a form or booklet of information about your child, including their likes and dislikes, comfort items and special people in their lives, so they can start to get to know them before the childcare arrangement starts. Some may request photos of family members and favourite things, to help them learn all about your little one and to talk about with your child if they seem to be pining for you. And some like to do a home visit, so they can get to know your child in a situation where they feel completely comfortable.

You may find it helpful to ask the childcarer about their own hobbies and interests, to help your child get to know and start to bond with them. Some children find it reassuring to discover they have something in common with their new carer, whether it's a love of cats, a passion for dancing or a hatred of tomatoes!

If your child is in centre-based care, it's especially important to make sure they are bonding with their key worker. Throughout the settling-in process, get reassurance that the key worker is spending plenty of time with your child and making a special effort to welcome them. As your child gets older, you will probably need to go through parts of the settling-in process all over again as they move up to a new room with a new keyworker and staff team.

Leaving your child

Some children, especially very young babies and those of school age, are quite content to be left with someone else and won't be at all bothered when you leave. But for many, the prospect of being without mummy or daddy is distressing and it's quite normal to have tears when you go (possibly not just from the child!)

Most experts agree that it's best to explain to your child that you are leaving and when you will be returning, whether that's: 'I'm just popping out to post a letter, I'll be back in ten minutes,' during a settling-in session, or 'Mummy has to go work today, but I'll be back to pick you up before teatime' on a work day. Even babies not yet old enough to talk will understand some of what you are saying and feel reassured by your tone of voice.

Although it may seem easier, don't sneak off while your child is distracted, or pretend to be nipping to the loo when you're leaving for a full day. Your child may become confused and distressed when they realise you're not there, and distrustful of you and their carer.

Instead, keep your departure short and sweet. Dragging it out, or returning after you've already said goodbye, will confuse your child and probably upset both of you more. Your childcarer will be very used to settling children after a tearful or sullen parting, and you can help by suggesting some things that may help to occupy and calm your little one, such as a favourite song, snack or toy. Of course your instinct when your child is crying is to comfort them, and walking away always feels awful, compounding any guilt or uncertainty you're feeling about going back to work.

Rest assured that in a few minutes your child will probably be playing quite happily. Most carers won't mind if you phone or text several times a day during the early days to see how your child is getting on. Some may even send picture messages to reassure you that your little one has settled and show you all the fun they're having while you're at work.

If your child has a comfort item, such as a dummy, special blanket or cuddly toy, make sure this is in their bag and tell your childcarer about it. Some children may also be comforted by having something familiar that smells of mum or dad, such as a scarf or cardigan. Another tip for slightly older children is to give them something of yours to look after, such as a pair of gloves or a glasses case, until you return. Knowing that you've left something important reassures your child that you'll come back for it – and them.

Try to keep your child's home life consistent and stable while they are getting used to a new childcare arrangement. This isn't the best time to be potty training, withdrawing a dummy or moving to a grown-up bed. A healthy diet and plenty of sleep should also help your child be on good form to cope with this big change in their lives.

Separation anxiety

By around the age of six months, babies start to learn the concept of 'object permanence', ie that something can exist even when it is out of sight (which is why games of peek-a-boo are such a delight for this age group). They're also discovering that they are individuals, separate from their primary caregiver (usually mum), and getting better at recognising different faces and distinguishing those that are familiar from those that are unfamiliar. Soon after, at around seven to eight months, most babies start to experience separation anxiety. They may become anxious and start to cry if mum goes out of sight, even for just a few seconds, and get distressed if they can't see a familiar face. Separation anxiety tends to peak at around ten to twelve months and gradually eases after around eighteen months. This six- to eighteen-month window is exactly when many mothers in the UK return to work. Leaving your young child at any age is a huge pull, and separation anxiety makes it especially heart-wrenching.

There's no way of avoiding separation anxiety, but rest assured that it is very common and a positive sign that your baby is developing normally and the two of you have a strong relationship. Your baby or toddler should soon form a secure attachment with their childcarer, discover that they are safe, well looked after and have fun while in their care, and learn that you always come back. Then the separation anxiety will fade – and you may find instead that you have tears because they don't want to come home!

Building a good relationship with your childcarer

You and your daycare provider are partners in your child's care, education and welfare. Developing a strong, mutually supportive relationship with them will give you peace of mind while at work and, most importantly, help your child to thrive in their care.

Your responsibilities in the childcare arrangement should be clearly defined in the contract you've agreed with your childcarer. Build trust and respect by always meeting these, which in practice generally means:

- being punctual with drop-offs and pick-ups
- always paying fees and expenses on time and in full
- supplying any food, clothing or equipment you've agreed to provide
- giving as much notice as possible of any changes your childcare requirements, whether you've booked a holiday for next summer or your train's running late that evening
- adhering to rules and policies, especially the sickness policy (no matter how inconvenient this may be).

Good communication is crucial, so make time to talk with your childcarer, both informally and at formal reviews. In particular, always let your childcarer know if there's anything that might have an impact on your child's mood or behaviour – for example a disturbed night's sleep, new teeth coming through, recent immunisations, or any kind of upheaval at home.

Re-assess the childcare arrangement periodically, discussing what's going well and anything that could be improved. If it's difficult to chat when children are present, try an evening meet-up or phone conversation. Sharing information about your little one's latest likes, dislikes, obsessions, fears, achievements and eccentricities will help your care provider to plan activities that engage and stimulate your child, and keep them safe and content.

Many childcare settings give parents a daily review sheet, especially if the child is too young to talk about their day. These typically include information about what the child has been doing, as well as details of food and drink consumed, naps, nappy changes/toileting, and any observations about their development or behaviour. Some providers prefer this to be a two-way process, with each child having a diary in which both carer and parents can note information and observations.

If your childcarer hasn't yet mentioned this sort of information-exchange, ask about it when your child starts attending. Increasingly, childcare professionals are using password-protected online systems, through which they can record your child's progress, share policies, process invoices, and email you record forms.

It's important that your childcarer knows what you expect of them, but make sure these expectations are realistic. A nanny can't fill your child's day with educational activities, while at the same time tackling the huge ironing pile and preparing a gourmet three-course-meal. A nursery worker might not be able to spend hours coaxing your child to eat a food they're not keen on when they have to make sure seven other children are eating their lunch too.

What if my child doesn't settle?

It generally takes children several days or even weeks to get used to any sort of daycare situation, and during this time you may find you have to contend with tears, sulkiness, despondency, aggression or disrupted sleeping and eating patterns. This behaviour should subside as your little one becomes accustomed to the new arrangement, starts to enjoy the new activities and company it provides, and learns that mum or dad always come back at the end of the day.

In the meantime, do everything you can to make the childcare set-up enjoyable for your child. Pack some favourite toys or books in their bag, put favourite foods in their lunchbox, promise a favourite story or trip to the park at the end of the day, and enjoy some quality time together doing favourite activities on non-childcare days. It might also be helpful for the childminder or nursery key worker to visit your child at home, so they can get to know each other one-to-one in familiar surroundings. Ask your childcarer for advice too – they probably have experience of dealing with similar situations. If, after two or three months, your child still seems unhappy, you might want to consider changing provider, and possibly changing the type of childcare too.

What if I have concerns?

If you are at all concerned about any aspect of the childcare provision, raise it with your childcarer as soon as possible. It's always best to discuss little gripes before they become big grumbles, and any good childcare provider will want to listen to and learn from parents' feedback.

If you're not happy with the way the matter has been dealt with, you might want to take it up a level: to the nursery's manager, your nanny's agency, or your childminder's network co-ordinator or agency manager if they have one. Registered settings should have a complaints policy, with information about how to contact the registering body (eg Ofsted in England) with a serious complaint. **If you have any urgent concerns about children's safety or welfare, contact your local social services department, the police or the NSPCC straight away.**

What if my child becomes more attached to their carer than to me?
They won't! Even if your child is in full-time childcare, five days a week, no one will ever replace their mum or dad. Your child will always understand that you are their parents and the most important people in their lives.

Love isn't a finite resource that is divided up and shared out. Rather it's something that multiplies with each new loving relationship that's formed. Encouraging your child to develop a close bond with their childcarer is a positive thing to do, and great preparation for developing further strong and loving relationships as they grow older.

And don't forget...
Caring for young children is a hugely responsible and demanding profession. Let your childcarer know how much you appreciate their hard work by giving thanks and praise when deserved, and occasional gifts and treats.

Juggling work (or studying) and parenthood

Being a parent is a full-time job. Adding work or studying into the equation, whether full time or part time, will probably demand levels of organisation and planning unknown in your life pre-children.

The first few weeks as a working parent can be exhausting, particularly if you are still breastfeeding or having disturbed nights. You'll probably have a lot to catch up on in your job and, however wonderful your childcare arrangement, your child may take some time to get used to their new carer and routine. Make things easier for yourself by finding practical ways of making life run as smoothly as possible. Here are a few ideas:

- Unless you're a dynamo in the mornings, prepare as much as you can the night before: clothes for you and baby; packed lunches; petrol or travel pass; breakfast things; childcarer's diary or handover notes; a fully-packed changing bag; even coats and shoes.
- You may find it easier and quicker to get yourself fully ready before waking your child.

- Once dressed, slip a lightweight dressing gown or oversized shirt over your work clothes. That way, if your little one covers you in porridge, toothpaste (or worse!) you won't have to worry about finding a change of outfit.
- Keep a stock of healthy breakfast foods that either of you can eat 'on the go' when your morning routine doesn't quite go to plan.
- If you've been on maternity or parental leave, you've probably taken on more of the household chores and errands while you've been at home, and it's important to find a fair balance when you go back to work. Discuss with your partner how you're going to divide the day-to-day cooking, housework, laundry, grocery shopping and children's admin when you're both working. If you can afford it, you might want to consider paid help.
- You probably won't feel like cooking every night after work, so make meals in batches and freeze, use a slow cooker if it suits you, and don't feel bad about relying on ready meals and takeaways when you need to.
- Automate your finances as much as possible, so that bills (including childcare fees) and credit cards are all paid by direct debit.
- Supermarket delivery or 'click and collect' services are a great time-saver – you can automatically add all the things you need every week to your online basket and do your grocery shopping from your desk or on the train.
- Bulk-buy birthday cards and gifts, so that you don't have to stress about finding them at the last minute.
- Make your work wardrobe as low-maintenance as possible. Think twice about clothes that need ironing, hand-washing or dry-cleaning. Check the weather forecast for a few days ahead, then prepare several outfits for yourself and your child in one go.
- Try to keep your home life calm and consistent for the first few months after going back to work. This is probably not the best time to be moving house or building an extension.
- Read your company's family and childcare policies. Some

– especially larger firms in higher earning professions – offer extras such as emergency nannies or crèches, nanny payroll management, parenting seminars or parents' sabbaticals.

It's important to look after yourself too, physically, mentally and emotionally, as you adjust to life as a working parent. Life can feel frantic and pressures relentless, especially after a lengthy spell of parental leave, and you may feel divided loyalties as you strive to meet the needs of your family and your employer.

- Be upfront about your expectations, with your childcarer, partner, children, and colleagues. If you're not happy about something, say so.
- Don't compare yourself or your work-life set-up unfavourably with others. Every parent is doing the best they can for their family. Remind yourself from time to time of all the positive things about your own work situation and family life.
- Negative news stories about childcare may make you feel anxious or guilty, but try not to worry. You've done everything possible to ensure your child will be safe, happy and well cared for while you're at work, and you will know if the choice you've made is right for your family.
- You might want to book a holiday not too long after returning to work, so you have a break to look forward to.
- Try to find some time in the week when you're not a worker or a parent, but just you. Enjoy some exercise, a hobby, meeting friends, a 'date-night' with your partner, or simply switching off and relaxing in a warm bath or in front of a favourite TV show.
- Time with your children becomes more precious when you're working, so make the most of it. And keep photos of your children in your workplace, wallet and phone to remind yourself what it's all about.

What parents say...

'Have multiple back-up options in place. It can be hard when you're a new parent in a new area, but it's important that when plan A goes wrong (which it envitably will sometimes), you can go straight to plan B or C. If my nanny is ill, I call on a local childminder I met through a babysitting agency, and if all else fails my in-laws will step in.'
– *Lara, management consultant and mother of one*

'The first six weeks or so will always be tough, settling your child in and getting to grips with it all. Don't despair and try to give everything a good three months before deciding it isn't working. Although continuity is ideal, if something isn't right don't be afraid to change it.'
– *Emily, solicitor and mother of two*

'Don't worry about your children when you're at work. They will be happy and adapt to their new carer and situation. (Even if it doesn't appear to be the case at first when you drop them off and leave them screaming!) I love having the mix of adult interaction and "me" time (and being able to use my brain again!), when I'm at work, as well as spending quality time with my children on my non-working days.'
– *Kerry, senior hydrologist and mother of two*

'I feel I'm in the middle of set of scales with "good employee" on one side and "good mother" on the other. There's pressure, expectation and guilt on both sides, and I'm constantly trying to keep the whole thing balanced. Do I get it right all the time? No! But I do think I'm a better mother for being a working parent. And I think my company benefits from having a loyal and dedicated member of staff who's as flexible with them as they are with me.'
– *Alison, human resources manager and mother of two*

Further information

What's the difference between an NNEB and an NVQ? What do the tabloids mean by 'the nappy curriculum'? How does a Montessori nursery differ from other nurseries? If you're not sure, read on for some handy background information that might prove useful when you're researching your childcare options and questioning possible providers.

1 Childcare qualifications

2 The Early Years Foundation Stage

3 Childcare approaches and philosophies

4 Useful contacts

1. Childcare qualifications

There's a bewildering array of qualifications that a childcare provider may include on their CV or mention at an interview. Finding out exactly what your would-be childcarer has studied, where, when, and to what level, will help you decide whether they are the right person to care for your child.

Since the early 2000s there has been a huge amount of government effort and investment devoted to 'up-skilling' the childcare workforce. The thinking is that better qualified childcare professionals will be better able to ensure children's wellbeing, prepare them for school and ultimately improve their life chances – especially for disadvantaged youngsters and those in need. Other advantages of having common skills, knowledge and standards across the sector are more consistency, improved communication and enhanced status for childcare workers.

Which level?

All vocational qualifications in England, Wales and Northern Ireland are now part of the Qualifications and Credit Framework (QCF), which covers qualifications up to level 4. It is broadly aligned with the Framework for Higher Education Qualifications, which covers levels 4 to 8.

These levels are set out in the QCF for England and Northern Ireland, and the Credit and Qualifications Framework for Wales (CQFW). Scotland has a different system made up of 12 levels of qualification, defined in the Scottish Credit and Qualifications Framework (SCQF). There is also a European Qualifications Framework (EQF), which largely mirrors the QCF and should help you to understand how qualified your childcarer is if they have done their training elsewhere in Europe.

Which subject?

Childcare professionals generally study for awards, certificates and diplomas in subjects such as: early years care and education; early learning; children's care, learning and development; childhood studies;

NB: this is not a fully comprehensive list, and childcare qualifications are subject to frequent change.

Level	Suitable for	Examples of old qualifications	Examples of current qualifications
Entry	Childcarers with no previous experience		• Entry level awards, certificates and diplomas
1 (broadly equivalent to GCSE grade D to G standard)	All childcarers		• Level 1 awards, certificates and diplomas • Certificates in first aid, food hygiene and child protection
2 (broadly quivalent to GCSE A* to C standard)	Childcarers who work under supervision (eg nursery assistants)	NVQ level 2	• Level 2 awards, certificates & diplomas • Intermediate apprenticeships • BTEC level 2
3 (broadly equivalent to A level standard)	Childcarers who work unsupervised, eg nannies, nursery room leaders, childminders	NNEB NVQ level 3	• Any level 3 qualification with 'Early Years Educator' (EYE) in the title • Advanced apprenticeships • BTEC level 3 • HBCA or CYPOP5 for childminders
4	Childcare managers and professionals who want to develop their careers	NVQ level 4	• Certificate of higher education
5	As above	NVQ level 5	• Foundation degree • Higher National Diploma
6 (degree level)	Compulsory for leaders of maintained (ie state-funded) nurseries	Early Years Professional Status	• Bachelor's degree • Early Years Teacher Status (EYTS) *
7			• Master's degree • PGCE and other postgraduate certificates
8			• Doctorate

*EYTS is not currently considered equivalent to Qualified Teacher Status (QTS), although many in the early years world are campaigning for it to be and argue that teachers in early years settings should earn the same as their counterparts in school reception classes.

nursery nursing; children and young people; caring for children; or home-based childcare – amongst others. Qualifications in playwork are best suited to those working with school-aged children.

How much study?

A qualification at any level may be called an 'award', a 'certificate' or a 'diploma', depending on how much study is involved. All qualifications on the QCF are made up of credits, with each credit equating to around ten hours' work:

Award = 1 – 12 credits
Certificate = 13 – 36 credits
Diploma = 37+ credits

So a childcarer who has a diploma has studied in more depth than one with a certificate, and one with a certificate could undertake further studies to upgrade to a diploma.

What sort of learning?

Childcare qualifications may involve classes at college, distance learning from home, or practical training on the job – often a mixture of these. You might want to ask your prospective childcarer what the balance was in their training.

Beware of qualifications that a childcarer has achieved solely through distance learning or online study, with no assessment of their practice in the workplace. They may be delivered by unscrupulous online training providers and not included on the Government's list of 'full and relevant' childcare qualifications.

Which awarding body?

There are dozens of different awarding bodies for childcare qualifications. Among the best known are the Council for Awards in Children's Care and Education (CACHE) and City & Guilds (C&G).

Most C&G courses and many CACHE ones are studied by workers in the course of their regular job. BTEC vocational qualifications, which are usually undertaken by college students wanting to get into a childcare career, are all awarded by Pearson Edexcel.

Many universities and colleges (including the Open University) offer their own childcare qualifications. The Montessori Centre International delivers specialist qualifications in Montessori education, and the famous Norland College has its own degree programme and diploma for nannies.

Any specialisms?

Some qualifications include optional modules in particular areas of child-care, such as caring for young babies, playwork or working with children who have special needs. You might want to ask your would-be childcarer if they have any specialist training or areas of professional interest.

Recent developments

In September 2014, new measures came into place in England to further raise professionalism among early years workers, and to make early years qualifications easier to understand:

- Level 3 qualifications that are considered by the Government to be 'full and relevant' for professionals working in the early years sector now all have the words 'Early Years Educator' in their title.
- Anyone doing an Early Years Educator qualification must also have at least a grade 'C' in GCSE English and maths by the time they complete their course. Those with the qualification but without these GCSES may not be counted as a level 3 staff member in their workplace.

These rules are not being applied retrospectively, so for the time being you may still come across level 3 qualified childcarers without a grade C or higher in GCSE maths or English.

Older qualifications

Many people have heard of the NNEB (National Nursery Examination Board), which delivered the standard qualification for nannies and nursery nurses until 1994, when it merged with the Council for Early

Years Awards to form CACHE. The NNEB has long been superseded by other level 3 qualifications (such as the CACHE Level 3 Diploma in Early Years Education and Care [Early Years Educator]), but many mature nannies and nursery workers still proudly promote their NNEB status.

A large number of childcare professionals have National Vocational Qualifications (NVQs) at levels 2–5. Workers studied for NVQs in the course of their regular job, but the qualifications have been phased out since 2010, being replaced by QCF qualifications (see page 182). Their equivalent in Scotland, Scottish Vocational Qualifications, still exist.

You can check whether your childcarer's qualification is on the list of those deemed 'full and relevant' for early years workers at: **www.education.gov.uk/eypqd/qualifications.shtml** Be aware that childcare qualifications often have very similar names. If you don't see an exact match, then your childcarer's qualification is not on the list.

Continuing professional development (CPD)

You may want to ask your prospective childcarer at interview whether they plan to do further training. If they do, it's a good sign that they are committed to their childcare career, and your children may benefit from their new skills and knowledge.

If you employ a nanny or au pair, you can support them by giving them time, space and encouragement to pursue their studies. All childcarers will appreciate your interest in their professional development and your cooperation with any assignments and observations they have to carry out.

Childcarers who are members of the Professional Association for Childcare and Early Years (PACEY) commit to doing at least 15 hours of CPD each year.

The most important qualifications...

Research by the Family and Childcare Trust, Oxford University and others, suggests that, although parents value a childcare professional's ability to deliver stimulating educational activities and monitor their child's development, they value life experience and personal qualities more. Despite the laudable drive for a better qualified childcare workforce, it seems that what parents want most of all is a childcarer who's loving and caring.

Further information

Find out more about qualifications for childcare professionals at:
www.gov.uk/early-years-qualifications-finder
www.bapn.org.uk/Parents_Advice.aspx
www.accreditedqualifications.org.uk
www.cache.org.uk

Wales
www.ccwales.org.uk/edrms/140232/

Scotland
www.gov.scot
(search for 'childcare qualifications')

Northern Ireland
www.nidirect.gov.uk/guide-to-qualifications

2. The Early Years Foundation Stage

Often described in the press as 'the nappy curriculum', the Early Years Foundation Stage (EYFS) framework is a set of standards that describes how professionals in England working with children from birth to the age of five should support their development, learning and welfare.

The EYFS is a play-based curriculum, as research shows that young children learn most effectively through play. It is followed by all daycare nurseries and registered childminders, as well as by staff in preschools and primary school reception classes. Nannies, au pairs and other forms of care that aren't compulsorily inspected by Ofsted don't have to follow the EYFS.

Among the requirements of the EYFS is that every child in every childcare setting should have a 'key person' with lead responsibility for their care and welfare. The EYFS also includes guidance on making sure the childcare environment has suitable facilities and equipment, and that staff are suitable to work with children. It covers young children's learning and development too, across seven areas:
  - personal, social and emotional
  - communication and language
  - physical development
  - reading and writing
  - mathematics
  - understanding of the world
  - expressive art and design.

Practitioners working with the youngest children will focus most strongly on the first three year of these, called the 'prime areas'.

Your childcare provider will keep records of your child's progress within the EYFS. You'll receive written summaries at the ages of two and five, but you can ask to see your child's records at any time. You should find that monitoring your child's progress according to the EYFS is a two-way process, with your childcarer sharing information with you, asking about your child's development at home, and both of you giving each other ideas to support your child's learning.

The EYFS recognises that every child is unique and that all children develop at different rates and learn in different ways. Allowing for this, if any aspect of your child's development gives your childcarer cause for concern they will raise this with you and discuss whether your child might benefit from some specialist support.

This is just a brief overview of the EYFS. You'll find lots more information at:
www.foundationyears.org.uk
www.gov.uk/early-years-foundation-stage

The EYFS applies to England only. Other parts of the UK have their own standards and guidance for early years care and education.
Wales has the Early Years Foundation Phase:
www.gov.wales/topics/educationandskills/earlyyearshome/?lang=en
www.pacey.org.uk/childminders/in_wales/foundation_phase.aspx

Scotland has the Pre-birth to Three Guidance , Building the Ambition guidance and Curriculum for Excellence
www.educationscotland.gov.uk/earlyyears/index.asp
www.gov.scot/Resource/0045/00458455.pdf
www.gov.scot/Topics/People/Young-People/early-years

And Northern Ireland has Learning to Learn – a Framework for Early Education and Learning:
www.deni.gov.uk/articles/learning-learn
www.early-years.org

3. Early Years approaches and philosophies

Some nurseries, childminders, and nannies follow a particular educational philosophy or approach to learning, and many more childcare professionals are trained in, or influenced by, such methodologies. Here are some of the approaches you may come across during your search for childcare.

Montessori

Montessori settings adhere to the work of the groundbreaking Italian physician and educator Dr Maria Montessori (1870–1952). Dr Montessori was a pioneer of child-centred learning and believed that young children, especially up to the age of six, have periods when they are particularly sensitive to acquiring new skills and learning new things. Her approach aims to make the most of these learning windows, and to help children become independent and self-motivated learners.

Hallmarks of a Montessori establishment include:

- an ordered environment where children can freely access materials and resources without adult help
- large, mixed-age groupings where children of different ages can teach and learn from one another
- an emphasis on sensory learning, including in the natural world and using specially designed Montessori resources
- children learning practical life skills, such as pouring, whisking and polishing, and doing real-life activities, such as washing, cleaning and cooking
- long blocks of uninterrupted work/activity time, typically lasting three hours
- a calm, unhurried and harmonious atmosphere, with staff and children who are polite, courteous and respectful

- competition and testing kept to a minimum
- staff trained in the Montessori ethos.

Find out more at:

www.montessori.org.uk

www.montessorisociety.org.uk

Steiner Waldorf

Steiner Waldorf education is based on the work of the Austrian philosopher, architect, playwright and social reformer Rudolf Steiner (1861–1925). It offers a holistic approach, emphasising children's creative, spiritual and moral development alongside their academic education.

In a Steiner setting you're likely to find:

- an emphasis on oral storytelling, poetry, rhymes, singing and recitation, to encourage listening and speech development
- lots of painting, drawing, crafts and dance to encourage artistic expression
- puppets and blank-faced dolls to support the development of children's imaginations
- a gentle environment, with no 'hard' corners or bright colours, and furniture and toys made from natural materials
- children in mixed age groups, engaged in practical domestic activities such as cooking, sewing, cleaning and caring for animals
- children working with natural materials such as clay, wood, beeswax and sheep's wool
- lots of outdoor activities
- organic meals and snacks
- little or no adult interference in play
- young children's work not displayed (the focus is on the process, not the end product)
- no formal literacy or numeracy (children in Steiner schools don't begin formal education until around the age of seven)
- no TVs, computers or other electronic gadgets (these aren't introduced in Steiner education until children reach adolescence).

Early Years settings in England that follow the Steiner philosophy are exempt from following the parts of Early Years Foundation Stage framework that conflict with their ethos. They do not have to meet the literacy Early Learning Goals, nor the EYFS assessment requirements, and they work towards modified Early Learning Goals in areas such as mathematics and technology.

As well as the schools that bear his name, Rudolf Steiner founded a spiritual philosophy called Anthroposophy ('knowledge of the human being'), which encompasses theories on the occult, reincarnation, science, medicine and more. Although Anthroposophy is not taught explicitly as a subject or theory in Steiner schools, it underpins Steiner educators' training and research, and is something you might want to look into further if this style of education interests you.

Find out more about Steiner education at:
www.steinerwaldorf.org

Reggio Emilia

The Reggio Emilia approach to daycare and preschool education was developed by teacher Loris Malaguzzi (1920–1994), working in the villages around the city of Reggio Emilia in Italy after the Second World War. Malaguzzi believed that children have the desire and ability to construct their own knowledge, as well as endless ways of expressing themselves. He saw Reggio Emilia settings as a partnership between parents, teachers and the local community.

Features of a Reggio Emilia setting include:
- teachers in the role of 'researchers' and 'co-learners', taking notes, photos and recordings of what children are doing, thinking and feeling, and regularly discussing their observations with colleagues
- children encouraged to express themselves in a huge range of different ways, for example through art, sculpture, drama, dance, song, storytelling or emergent writing (Reggio Emilia calls these different forms of expression the '100 languages of children')
- project-based learning, with children supported to pursue their

own interests and to discuss them in depth
- a practical and multi-sensory approach to learning, with children engaged in activities such as gardening and woodwork, or using materials such as sand and clay
- the physical environment seen as an additional teacher, with attractive resources accessible to children and frequently rearranged
- lots of plants and natural light, to bring a sense of the outdoors into the building
- a large studio/workshop called an 'atelier' for group activities
- an open kitchen, with nutritious food prepared on-site and mealtimes seen as a fun, social and educational experience
- displays of children's work, photos, and transcripts of their comments
- lots of mirrors on walls and ceilings to help children see themselves and their activities from different perspectives
- natural materials and 'found objects', such as pebbles, fir cones, shells and buttons
- parents welcomed as partners, collaborators and advocates in their children's learning
- no manuals, guides, curriculum or tests.

Find out more at:
www.reggiochildren.it

HighScope

The HighScope approach was founded by Dr David Weikart (1931–2003), a teacher who by the 1960s had become director of special services in Ypsilanti, Michigan. Concerned about the educational and social outcomes of 'at risk' children from poor families, he set up the Perry Hill Preschool Study. This followed two groups of these underprivileged children, 58 who were randomly assigned to the HighScope project and 65 who did not attend a preschool setting, for over 40 years. The HighScope group had vastly betters outcomes throughout their lives, with higher IQs, better qualifications, higher earnings, less criminality, and so on.

Dr Weikart believed that children build their knowledge of the world through hands-on practical experiences. In creating the HighScope approach, he drew on the work of 'constructivist' educational theorists such as Jean Piaget, John Dewey and Lev Vygotsky.

Characteristics of a HighScope setting include:

- defined areas (eg home corner, block play, art, sand and water), with resources clearly displayed and accessible to children
- the 'plan-do-review' method: children choose the materials they want to use, discuss how they plan to use them, carry out their plan, then reflect on whether it was as they expected or not
- staff as facilitators, rather than managers or supervisors. Adults support or validate what children already know, then encourage and challenge them to take their learning to the next level.
- squabbles and arguments resolved calmly without punishment or isolation. Instead the children involved are encouraged to explain the problem and come up with ideas to resolve it.
- staff recording each day things that children do or say, and reviewing these anecdotes periodically as a measure of development
- staff monitoring children's progress against 58 key developmental indicators in eight areas of learning
- sensitivity to children's non-educational needs (including medical, financial and social)
- parents and families encouraged to get involved, and seen as partners in their children's learning.

Find out more at:

www.highscope.org

Forest Schools

The Forest Schools movement takes its inspiration from woodland schools and kindergartens set up in Wisconsin, USA, in the 1920s, and in Scandinavia and Germany in the mid-20th century. In a Forest School early years setting, children regularly spend extended periods of time in a specially prepared area of local woodland. Although many early years settings now involve children in woodland activities, only those whose staff are qualified Forest School practitioners should use the Forest School name.

This outdoor, child-led approach to play and education involves lots of problem-solving, teamwork, observation and physical challenges, and so helps develop children's physical, practical, intellectual and social skills. Children who struggle with academic environments or social constraints, such as those with ADHD or autism, often thrive in Forest School settings.

A Forest School setting is normally a clearing – natural or man-made – in woodland. Sites vary hugely, but you're likely to find:

- adult-prepared areas, such as a permanent shelter, fire pit, rope swing, tool store, or circle of seating for stories and songs
- child-initiated activities, for example making mud pies, building shelters, playing in fallen leaves, observing insects or making environmental art
- children encouraged to take 'supported risks' through activities such as building and lighting fires, damming streams, climbing trees and sliding on mud or ice
- no commercially produced toys or play equipment
- the site used all year round, in all weathers (Forest School sites are only out of bounds if deemed dangerous, for example during a flood or gale)
- all children and staff in appropriate clothing and footwear to protect against the elements
- drinks and snacks served outdoors
- staff specially trained as Forest School practitioners
- risk-assessments carried out daily, before children enter the site
- children taking something away with them at the end of each session to encourage parental interest and ongoing discussion.

Find out more at:

www.forestschools.com
www.forestschoolassociation.org

4. Useful contacts

This is a selection of the organisations referred to in this book. It is not a comprehensive list. The commercial organisations are not endorsed by the author or publisher, and their inclusion is not advertising.

Childcare organisations

4Children
www.4children.org.uk 020 7512 2112
www.foundationyears.org.uk

British Association of Professional Nannies (BAPN) www.bapn.org.uk 01622 815271

British Au Pair Agencies Association (BAPAA)
www.bapaa.org.uk

Family and Childcare Trust
www.familyandchildcaretrust.org
020 7940 7510

National Day Nurseries Association
www.ndna.org.uk 01484 407070

Northern Ireland Childminding Association
www.nicma.org 028 9181 1015

Out of School Alliance
www.outofschoolalliance.co.uk 01638 744056

Pre-school Learning Alliance
www.pre-school.org.uk 020 7697 2500

Professional Association for Childcare and Early Years (PACEY)
www.pacey.org.uk 0300 003 0005

Scottish Childminding Association
www.childminding.org
01786 449063

Scottish Family Information Service
www.scottishfamilies.gov.uk

For organisations relating to children with additional needs, see pages 146–147.

Support for working families

Acas
www.acas.org.uk 0300 123 1100

Citizens Advice
www.citizensadvice.org.uk

The Fatherhood Institute
www.fatherhoodinstitute.org 0845 634 1328

Grandparents Association
www.grandparents-association.org.uk
0845 4349585

Tax Credits Helpline
www.gov.uk/tax-credits-calculator
0345 300 3900

Working Families
www.workingfamilies.org.uk 0300 012 0312

Regulation and inspection

Care and Social Services Inspectorate Wales
www.cssiw.org.uk 0300 7900 126

Care Inspectorate (Scotland)
www.scswis.com 0345 600 9527

Education Training Inspectorate (N Ireland)
www.etini.gov.uk 028 9127 9726

Estyn (Wales)
www.estyn.gov.wales 029 2044 6446

Ofsted (England)
www.ofsted.gov.uk 0300 123 123
www.reports.ofsted.gov.uk

Disclosure & Barring Service (DBS)
www.gov.uk/government/organisations/
disclosure-and-barring-service 03000 200 190

Commercial organisations

Association of Nanny Agencies (ANA)
www.anauk.org

Au Pair World
www.aupairworld.com

Childcare.co.uk
www.childcare.co.uk

Daynurseries.co.uk
www.daynurseries.co.uk 01488 68432

Find A Babysitter
www.findababysitter.com

Morton Michel Insurance
www.mortonmichel.com 020 8603 09003

Mumsnet
www.mumsnet.com

Nannyjob
www.nannyjob.co.uk

Nanny Share
www.nannyshare.co.uk

Nannytax
www.nannytax.co.uk 0845 226 2203

Netmums
www.netmums.com

Norland Nannies
www.norland.co.uk 01225 904030

Safehands
www.safehandsbabysitters.com 0844 818 2810

Sitters
www.sitters.co.uk 08447 367367

Tinies
www.tinies.com

For a description of what each organisation offers, visit the book's website:
www.choosing-childcare.co.uk

The last word!

Becoming a working parent and finding the right childcare can feel almost as daunting and nerve-wracking as becoming a parent in the first place! I really hope the information and advice in this book have made the process a little easier and helped you to make the right decision for your family. You can keep up to date with the latest changes by visiting this book's accompanying website: **www.choosing-childcare.co.uk**. We'd love to know what you found most helpful, and anything you think needs updating or further explanation on the website.

I wish you and your family all the best for this new stage in your parenting adventure, and hope it proves enjoyable and rewarding for all of you.

Elyssa

Index